To
From

Marks and Spencer p.l.c.
Baker Street, London, W1U 8EP
www.marksandspencer.com

This book was created by The Complete Works

ISBN 1-84273-694-9
Printed in China

MARKS & SPENCER

First BIBLE Stories

Illustrated by John Dillow

THE OLD TESTAMENT

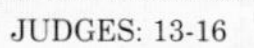

THE NEW TESTAMENT

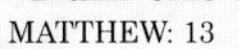

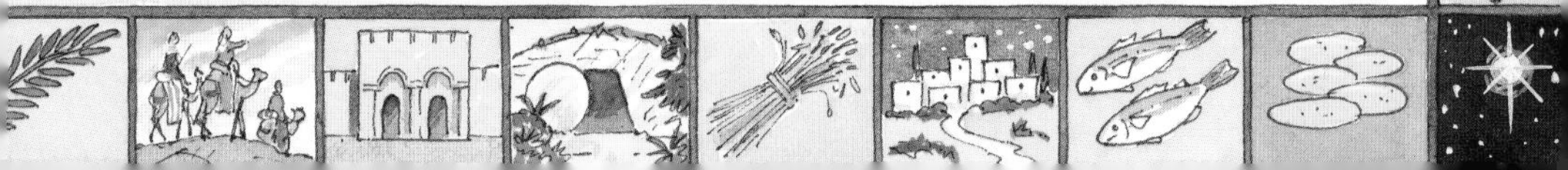

THE OLD TESTAMENT

And so the world began

GENESIS: 1-2

Long, long ago, before time began, there were no rivers or mountains, no streams or hills. There was nothing to see at all, nothing but darkness. But God was there and, into this darkness, God commanded light. So, the very first day began.

Then God started to make the seas…

and, in between the seas, He made dry land, covering it with all kinds of trees and plants.

Over all this, God placed a dazzling sun to shine by day...

and a shimmering moon to shine by night. He studded the sky with billions of twinkling stars...

and so the world began.

Then God filled the seas with fish of many colours. He added creeping crabs, sly sharks and huge, wallowing whales.

Above the land, He made birds soar and swoop, dip and loop. Beautiful butterflies, busy bees and bustling bats filled the air.

For the land areas, God made animals of every kind. He made them to gallop and trot, lope and hop.

Then God created the first man and woman, Adam and Eve, trusting them to care for all the creatures.

Everything was happy and contented. It had taken six days to complete this new world. God decided to rest on the seventh day, setting it apart and calling it the Sabbath.

No longer perfect

GENESIS: 2-3

In one special place, God laid out a garden for Adam and Eve to live in. It was full of lovely, lush plants and fantastic flowers. Sparkling streams bubbled up from the ground and every tree was covered with delicious fruit for Adam and Eve to eat.

So many different types of animals lived in the garden, that it took Adam many hours to give each one a name… gecko, gibbon, giraffe, gorilla, hare, hippo, horse, hyena…

Adam and Eve lived happily in the Garden of Eden, caring for it and the creatures that lived there. They had everything they needed.

In the centre of the garden grew a special tree. It was called the Tree of Knowledge. God made it very clear that this tree was different from all the other trees.

"You must not eat the fruit of this tree," God warned Adam and Eve. "You can eat fruit from all the others, but if you eat fruit from this one, bad things will happen."

And for a time, Adam and Eve did as they were told.

But there was a cunning snake living in the Garden of Eden, who wanted to play a trick on Eve.

One day, the snake saw Eve standing by the Tree of Knowledge. It slithered up to her, whispering softly, “Look at the lovely fruit.”

“I must not touch it,” said Eve.

“S-Smell how s-s-sweet it is,” the snake hissed.

“God told us to leave it alone,” Eve protested.

“Ha!” laughed the snake. “God doesn’t want you to know the things He does, the things that are good and the things that are evil!”

Eve looked at the delicious fruit, wondering what it would be like to know all that God knew. Reaching out, she picked a juicy-looking fruit and took a bite.

Then she passed it to Adam, for him to try. From that moment on, things started to go wrong.

When God spoke to Adam and Eve that night, He knew what they had done. He was angry and told them to leave the garden at once.

As Adam and Eve left, God sent an angel to stop them from returning.

While they had lived in the Garden of Eden, Adam and Eve had had everything they needed and they would never have grown old there. Now all that had changed. They had to work hard and knew that one day, they would die.

God's world was no longer perfect.

Two sons, Cain and Abel

GENESIS: 4

After they left the Garden of Eden, Adam and Eve had two sons, Cain and Abel. As they grew older, Cain worked on the land, growing food, while Abel took care of the sheep.

One day, the two brothers decided to offer some gifts to God. Cain gave food from his harvest, while Abel gave a lamb.

But God was only pleased with Abel's gift. He had looked into the hearts of both brothers and saw that Abel was good and honest, while Cain was evil and angry.

Cain was furious and, jealous of his brother, decided to kill him.

So, one day, Cain suggested to Abel that they should go walking. While they were out, Cain killed his brother. He thought no one had seen him, but God had.

When God asked Cain where Abel was, he lied and said, "I don't know."

"You have done a terrible thing," said God. "You cannot stay any more in this land."

"This punishment is too much," cried Cain. "You are driving me from my land and your presence. People will want to kill me for what I have done."

"No," said God, "I won't allow that to happen. I will make sure no one harms you."

Cain left his home, never to return and went to live in a land called "Wandering" for the rest of his life.

A fresh start

GENESIS: 6-9

As the years passed, God's people grew more and more evil. God looked at the world and saw that it was not as He had wanted it to be. He decided to put an end to it all. The world needed a fresh start.

God would send a huge flood to wash every bad thing away. But He intended to save Noah, who was a good, kind man, and his family.

God gave Noah very careful instructions and told him to prepare for the flood.

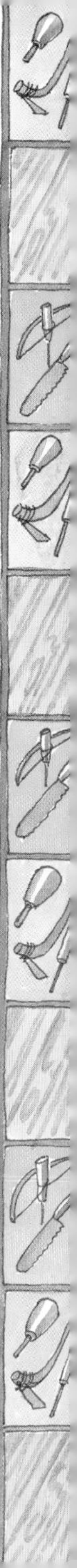

He told Noah to build an enormous boat, called an ark. Everyone laughed at Noah, because there was no open water for miles. But Noah ignored them.

For months, he went on building, until he had made an ark so huge, that it was as high as the tallest house.

When the boat was finished, Noah filled it with enough food to last for a very long time. Then, he gathered together two of every kind of animal in the world and led them into the ark. On and on stretched the queue, with creatures slithering and sliding, crawling and creeping, plodding and prancing, until, at last, they were all on board.

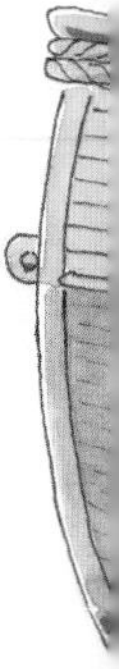

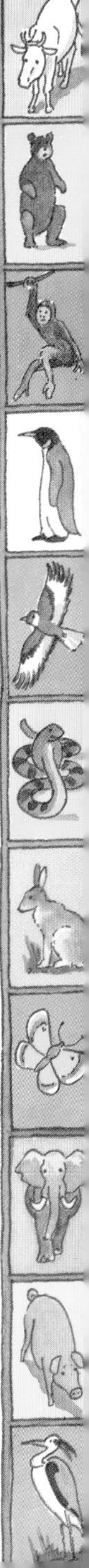

When Noah, his wife and the rest of Noah's family had joined them, God shut the door, tight and safe behind them.

It began to rain. Soft drizzle fell at first. Then, it began to fall faster and harder, beating down on the earth like on an enormous drum! Streams turned into rivers and rivers flowed into seas. And then the seas all joined together as one. The water spread and rose across God's earth, until there was not a single mountain top to be seen. All the people and animals drowned beneath the waves.

For forty days and forty nights, it rained and it rained and with nothing to see but water, the world felt a very sad and lonely place.

At last, the rain stopped and the waters began to go down. Noah opened a window and sent out a raven. But water still covered everything and the raven did not return.

Noah waited a while, then released a dove. But it soon came back, because the water was still too high.

When Noah tried again, the dove returned, carrying a bright, new olive leaf in its beak. Noah knew that the water was going down and that plants and trees must be growing again.

When Noah sent the dove out once more, it did not return. The flood had completely gone.

Noah opened the doors of the ark and the animals poured out onto the dry land.

"Never again will I destroy all living things by a flood," God promised Noah. "Whenever you see a rainbow in the sky, think of my promise and be sure that I will keep it."

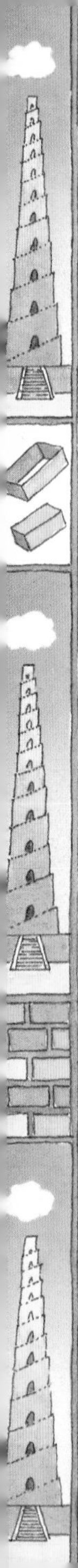

The tallest tower

GENESIS: 11

In the years after the great flood, Noah's family grew bigger and bigger and bigger. There were grandchildren, great-grandchildren and great-great-grandchildren. They began to fill all the corners of the world, as God had wanted them to do. The language that they all spoke, however, remained the same, so that everyone could still talk with one another.

One group made their home in a place called Babylonia. Slowly, they learned new skills, like how to make bricks. They used tar to stick the bricks together and built their homes with them.

One day, someone suggested that they should build the tallest tower that anyone had ever seen. This would make them famous all over the earth. So, work soon began.

God watched the walls of this tower grow higher and higher and He was very sad. He knew that this now meant that people only wanted to make themselves important and grand. They would think they were just as great as God. They would get bigger and bigger ideas and become as wicked as people were before the great flood.

God didn't waste any time. The people needed to be able to talk to each other in order to finish this tower. If they spoke in different languages and couldn't explain their ideas to one another, building would have to stop.

So, God made all his people speak in many languages and sent them to live in other countries around the world.

Father of a great nation

GENESIS: 12-13, 15, 18, 21

So it came about, that one of Noah's descendants, Abraham, settled in a place called Haran. Abraham was a good man, who believed in God. He and his wife, Sarah, were both quite old and had no children of their own.

One day, God told Abraham to leave the land that he thought of as home and move to a country called Canaan. "If you place your trust in me," God said, "I will make you the father of a great nation."

Abraham did trust God. So he packed up everything he owned and set off with Sarah, his servants and shepherds and his nephew, Lot, for an unknown land.

It was a difficult journey and it was many years before Abraham and his people finally settled in Canaan.

Things went well for a while, until one day, Abraham realised that there was not enough food and water for everyone. He agreed that Lot and his family should move to the lush lands below, while he and Sarah stayed where the ground was poorer.

When Lot had gone, God spoke to Abraham. "I will give you all the land you can see and it will be yours for ever," said God. "You will have as many children, grandchildren and great-grandchildren as there are stars in the sky. And you will be the father of a great nation that will last through the ages."

One day, a few years later, Abraham saw three men approaching him. Abraham offered them freshly baked bread, roasted meat, milk and cream.

After the meal, the men told Abraham and Sarah, "You will have a baby son in nine months." Sarah laughed – surely she was too old to have a child!

But nine months went by and God's promise came true. Sarah and Abraham had a son, Isaac. When he was born, Abraham recalled that God had told him that his children would form the beginnings of a great nation. Abraham knew that one day, this would be true.

The right wife for Isaac

GENESIS: 24

Time passed and Isaac grew up into a fine young man. After Sarah died, Abraham decided that Isaac should marry. He sent for his most trusted servant.

"You must go to my home country," said Abraham. "Find Isaac a wife. She must be someone from my own people."

"What if the girl doesn't want to come back here?" asked the servant. "Shall I take Isaac with me to your homeland?"

"No!" Abraham told him, firmly. "This land is part of God's plan for my people. If the girl won't come, return without her."

So, camels were loaded and the servant set out on the long journey.

At last, the servant arrived at the place where Abraham's brother, Nahor, lived. It was late in the afternoon and the camels were very tired. The servant settled the weary camels down to rest at the town well and began to pray.

"Please, God, help me to do what Abraham asked. Soon, the women will come to fetch water from the well. I shall ask one of them to give me a drink. If she is thoughtful enough to bring water for the camels, too, she will be the right wife for Isaac." Suddenly, the servant looked up and saw a beautiful girl, carrying a water jar.

The servant watched the girl fill her jar with water and then asked her for a drink. She gave him the jar and ran to fetch some water for his camels.

"Would it be possible," he asked, "for me to stay the night at your father's house?"

"I'm sure it would be," she replied, saying that she was Nahor's granddaughter, Rebecca. The servant thanked God for leading him straight to Abraham's family.

Rebecca ran home to tell everyone what had happened.

Her brother, Laban, welcomed the stranger and prepared food for him.

Then, the servant explained the reason for his journey and Rebecca's family understood that God intended Rebecca to be Isaac's wife.

Next morning, Abraham's servant was keen to set off for home. Although it meant leaving her family and going to live far away, Rebecca agreed to go with him. She said goodbye to everyone and then the two of them began the long journey back to Canaan.

It was evening time when Isaac first saw the train of camels approaching his home.

Isaac tried to listen to the old servant telling the story of his journey, but he hardly heard. He was too busy staring at the beautiful girl, who had travelled so far to be his wife.

They were married soon after and Isaac loved Rebecca very much.

The children of Israel

GENESIS: 25, 27-29, 32-33

Some time after Isaac and Rebecca were married, Rebecca gave birth to twin boys. They grew up very different to each other. Esau, the elder, who was Isaac's favourite, loved the outdoor life. He liked to hunt and often brought meat home from his hunting trips, which Isaac enjoyed eating in stews.

Jacob, the younger son and Rebecca's favourite, was much quieter. He preferred to stay at home.

Esau and Jacob even looked different. Jacob didn't have Esau's red hair or his brother's hairy skin.

As Isaac grew old, he went blind. He thought he might die soon. At that time, it was important that a dying father bless the oldest son, as the new head of the family. So, one day, Isaac sent Esau out hunting, so that they could share a meal of Isaac's favourite meat before the blessing.

Rebecca wanted Jacob to have the blessing. Isaac would never know if Jacob pretended to be his brother.

So, she made Isaac's favourite stew and dressed Jacob in Esau's clothes. She covered his arms with goatskin, to make them seem hairy like his brother's. Then, she sent him to Isaac with the food.

At first, all went well. Isaac smelled the delicious food. He reached out to his son and the feel of the hairy goatskin made him think it was Esau's arm that he was touching. But the voice sounded wrong.

"Are you really Esau?" Isaac asked his son.

"Yes, I am Esau," Jacob lied to his father.

So, Isaac prayed to God to bless Jacob, thinking that he was his oldest son.

When Esau returned and took food into his father, he learned the truth. Esau became so angry that Rebecca was afraid. She managed to persuade Isaac that it would be a good time for Jacob to seek a wife from their own people.

It was decided to send Jacob to stay with Rebecca's brother, Laban, until Esau had calmed down.

Jacob set off, feeling lonely and frightened. At sunset, he made camp in a valley and settled down to sleep. During the night, he had a dream. He saw a staircase reaching up to heaven, with angels moving up and down it. Then God spoke to Jacob, "I will give you and your children the land on which you lie. I will watch over you and look after you wherever you go."

When Jacob woke up, he was very afraid. A long journey to a strange land lay ahead of him. "If you protect me and bring me safely back home as you have said," Jacob prayed, "you will always be my God." Then, filled with renewed strength, he continued on the journey to his mother's country.

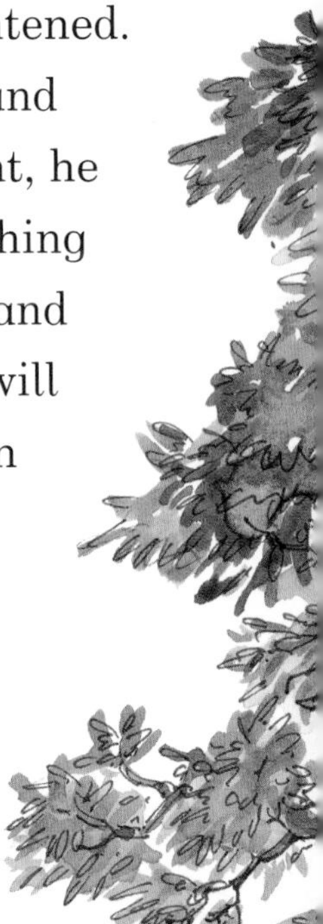

When Jacob finally arrived, he was made very welcome. He fell in love with Rachel, the youngest daughter of Laban. However, it was the custom for the oldest daughter to be married first, so Jacob took Leah, Rachel's sister, as his first wife. After some time, he also married Rachel.

Many years later, Jacob decided to return home to Canaan with his wives and family. But, on the way, he suddenly became afraid. How would Esau treat him? Would he be forgiven? So, Jacob sent messengers ahead, who returned with worrying news. Esau was on his way, with four hundred men.

Jacob chose various animals as presents for Esau, to be sent ahead with his servants. Alone in the camp, Jacob worried about his reunion with his brother and prayed to God for help. Suddenly, a stranger appeared and the two men began to wrestle. This stranger was God and had come to reassure Jacob that he was doing the right thing. When the stranger left, Jacob knew that he had been blessed and from that time on, he would be known as Israel.

When Jacob saw Esau approaching with his men, the trouble that he expected did not happen. Esau greeted his brother with open arms and all the old quarrels were forgotten.

"Seeing your welcoming face was like looking into the face of God," Jacob said, full of joy.

Many years later, Jacob's family came to be known as the children of Israel. God's promise had been fulfilled.

Sold for twenty silver pieces

GENESIS: 37

Jacob had twelve sons, ten with Leah and two – Joseph and Benjamin – with Rachel. Jacob's favourite was Joseph and he spoiled him. Because of this, the other brothers disliked Joseph. When their father gave Joseph a special coat, the brothers were very jealous.

Joseph made matters worse, because he insisted on telling everyone about his dreams, in which he was always the most important person.

In one dream, Joseph said that his brothers' sheaves of corn bowed down before his sheaf. "Do you think you are going to be king and rule over all of us?" asked his brothers. Joseph didn't answer.

One day, Jacob sent Joseph to see his brothers, who were looking after the sheep.

When the brothers saw Joseph approaching, they laid a plan to kill him. They would then throw his body into a deep, dry well and pretend that a wild animal had eaten him. They had had enough of Joseph and his dreams.

When Joseph arrived, the brothers seized him, but the oldest one, Reuben, persuaded them to think again. "Let us lower him into the well and leave him there to die," he said, planning to secretly rescue Joseph later.

Joseph could do nothing against so many of his brothers, as they ripped his coat from him and threw him into the deep, dark well.

A little later, as the brothers sat eating, some spice merchants passed by, on their way to Egypt. Seeing them, Judah had an idea.

"We won't gain anything if Joseph dies," he said. "Why don't we sell him as a slave?"

And so it was agreed. The terrified Joseph was dragged from the well and sold for twenty silver pieces to the next group of merchants who came along.

Then, the brothers killed a goat and smeared its blood on Joseph's coat.

When Jacob saw the torn coat, he was convinced that Joseph had been killed by a wild animal. He was heartbroken.

Meanwhile, in Egypt, the merchants had sold Joseph to Potiphar, the Captain of the Guard at the Pharaoh's court.

Thrown into prison

GENESIS: 39-41

Over the years, Joseph served Potiphar well. In time, he was put in charge of Potiphar's house and, later, all of his lands. But trouble was brewing.

Potiphar's wife was displeased with Joseph and told her husband lies, pretending that Joseph had attacked her. Potiphar had Joseph thrown into prison.

It just so happened that Pharaoh's butler and baker were also in the same jail. Joseph was given the job of serving these men.

One night, both of them had worrying dreams. "God can show us what dreams mean," said Joseph. "Tell me what you saw."

The butler told Joseph of a grapevine with three branches. He had squeezed the grape juice into Pharaoh's cup and given it to him to drink.

"The meaning is clear," said Joseph. "In three days, you will be free and back at work. Please, put in a good word for me."

Joseph turned to the baker. "You say that in your dream, you were carrying three baskets full of bread and pastries on your head and birds flew down and pecked at them."

Joseph shook his head, sadly. "This dream is not good," he said. "In three days, Pharaoh will kill you."

Joseph was right. Three days later, the butler was back at work in Pharaoh's palace and the baker was dead.

As soon as the butler was released, he forgot about the promise he had made and so Joseph remained in prison.

Two years later, Pharaoh's sleep was disturbed by strange dreams. In one dream, he was standing in a field by the River Nile, when seven plump, well-fed cows came out of the water and began to feed on the grass. These were followed by seven thin, bony cows, who ate up the first cows.

All the wisest men in Egypt couldn't help Pharaoh to understand what his dream meant. Then the butler remembered Joseph and mentioned him to Pharaoh. Joseph was instantly brought to the palace.

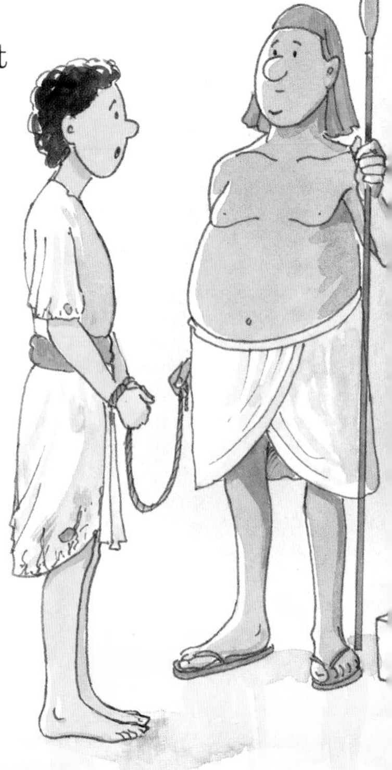

"There will be seven years of good harvests," explained Joseph. "After that, seven years of bad harvests will follow. You must store food in the good years, to help you through the bad."

Pharaoh could see that Joseph was a man of God. He was so impressed with him that he made Joseph his chief minister and gave him his own gold ring, a gold chain and fine clothes, as a mark of his new role.

Once again, everything happened just as Joseph predicted.

After Pharaoh, he was the most powerful man in Egypt and, because he had planned well, there was still plenty to eat when the years of famine came.

Reunited

GENESIS: 42-47

In Canaan, times were hard for Jacob and his family. He decided to send his sons, all except for Benjamin, to Egypt where corn was for sale.

So, Joseph's brothers stood before him and, not recognising him, asked if they might buy some corn. Joseph knew them at once and decided to see if they were still as cruel as they used to be.

Pretending to think they were spies, he had them thrown into prison.

Three days later, he told them to return home and bring back their youngest brother. Joseph loved Benjamin and very much wanted to see him again. Joseph kept one brother behind, to make sure that the others would return.

Joseph ordered his servants to fill his brothers' bags with corn, before they set off for home.

Back in Canaan, the brothers told Jacob everything, but he refused to let Benjamin go. He was terrified of losing another son.

Eventually, the corn ran out. Judah begged his father to let them return to Egypt, promising to look after Benjamin. Finally, Jacob agreed. And so the brothers came once again to Joseph, who had to fight back tears when he saw Benjamin.

"Is your father well?" he asked them. As they replied, they bowed low to him, just like the corn sheaves had bowed in Joseph's dream so many years before.

Joseph ordered food to be brought in and told the servants that Benjamin was to be given more than anyone else.

Then, the brothers' sacks were filled with food. This time, Joseph had his own silver cup hidden in Benjamin's bag. The brothers set off, but Joseph sent his guards after them, to look for the missing cup.

Horrified at the discovery of the cup, the brothers went back to Joseph and threw themselves at his feet.

“The man in whose sack my cup was found, must stay here as my servant. The rest of you can go!” Joseph commanded.

“Let me stay instead,” begged Judah. “Father will die of grief if Benjamin does not return.”

Now Joseph was sure that his brothers had changed. He sent the servants out of the room, burst into tears and announced, “I am Joseph!” His brothers stood shocked and terrified.

"It was God's plan that I was sent here to Egypt," Joseph told them, "so that I would be in a position to look after you when difficult times came. There are still five more years of famine to come. You must go home and bring the rest of the family here to live near me."

Joseph hugged Benjamin, then the rest of his brothers, as tears of joy streamed down his face.

So, Jacob and all of his family, the children of Israel, left Canaan and came to live in Egypt. There, Jacob was reunited with his much-loved son, Joseph.

Jacob settled comfortably in Goshen, the best part of Egypt and lived to be a great age.

You have been chosen

EXODUS: 1-4

While Joseph was alive, his people lived happily in Egypt, but after his death, things changed.

A new Pharaoh, who did not know how Joseph had helped Egypt during the famine, came to power. The new Pharaoh watched the Israelites grow in number. He became afraid that they would outnumber the Egyptians and be much more powerful.

He set them to work for him, making bricks and building new cities. Gradually, he turned them into the slaves of cruel Egyptian masters. Life became very difficult, but still the Israelite numbers grew. Finally, Pharaoh gave orders that any baby boy born to an Israelite family was to be killed.

At this time, an Israelite woman had a baby boy. While he was tiny and slept a lot, she managed to keep him hidden. But, after three months, this became difficult. He was beginning to make lots of noise!

The woman made a basket from reeds and waterproofed it by covering it with tar. Then, she placed her baby in it and with great care, hid it in the tall grasses at the edge of the river.

Her daughter, Miriam, stayed close by to watch. Soon, Pharaoh's daughter came to the river to bathe. She saw the basket and, as she looked into it, the baby began to cry. She realised that this was an Israelite boy and felt sorry for him.

Quickly, Miriam stepped forward. "Would you like me to find someone to look after the child for you?" she asked. Pharaoh's daughter agreed and, of course, Miriam ran to fetch her mother.

The mother looked after the baby, until he was old enough to live in Pharaoh's palace.

Pharaoh's daughter gave the boy the name of Moses. He was well cared for, but as he grew older, Moses never forgot that he was an Israelite. It greatly saddened him to see his people being treated so badly.

One day, Moses saw an Egyptian master kill an Israelite worker.

He leapt at the Egyptian and killed him. Moses knew that Pharaoh would hear of what he had done and he fled to the safety of the desert.

Moses went to live in a land called Midian, where he stayed for a long time, working as a shepherd.

One day, as he was watching over his flock, he noticed that a bush was on fire. Strangely, the bush remained whole. As he got nearer, Moses heard a voice, saying, "I am the God of Abraham and your ancestors. I have seen how the people of Israel are suffering. You are to go to Pharaoh and free my people."

"Please choose someone else," pleaded Moses. "No one will listen to me."

"You have been chosen," replied God. "Return to Egypt, find Aaron your brother, and go with him to ask Pharaoh to set my people free."

Let my people go

EXODUS: 5-14

Moses and Aaron went to Pharaoh and said, “The God of Israel says that you should let His people go.”

But Pharaoh didn't believe in God and became very angry. As a punishment, he made Moses' people work harder than ever.

"Give the Israelite slaves no more straw to make their bricks," he ordered. "Let them find their own. But they must make just as many bricks as before."

Moses went to tell God. "I will force Pharaoh to let my people go," said God. "Go and tell him that if he refuses again, dreadful things will happen."

Moses and Aaron returned to Pharaoh, determined to make him free the Israelites.

To show Pharaoh that they had been sent by God, Aaron threw his walking stick on the ground. Miraculously, it turned into a snake.

But Pharaoh's magicians could do the same and Pharaoh was not convinced. He refused to listen to Moses. So, God turned the waters of the River Nile into blood.

Then, frogs swamped the entire country. This was followed by swarms of gnats and flies. Only Goshen, the place where the Israelites lived, remained free of these things. But still, Pharaoh would not let the Israelites leave Egypt.

So, one by one, the Egyptian animals began to die, all except the ones in Goshen.

Even when the Egyptians became covered in boils, Pharaoh would not believe in God or set the Israelites free.

Then, God sent hail. It hailed like no one had ever seen before. Thundering hail, that beat down the crops and killed all of the remaining cattle.

Plagues of locusts followed, great humming swarms that ate every last green shoot, even the tiniest new leaf. At last, complete and total darkness covered the land and it remained that way for three whole days.

Pharaoh tried reasoning with Moses. But Moses insisted that all the Israelites, men, women, children and cattle, were freed – Pharaoh refused.

Then, late one night, God killed the eldest son of every Egyptian family, including Pharaoh's own son.

The Israelite families remained safe. God had told each family to kill a lamb or a goat and to splash a little of its blood on the doors to their homes. Then, they were to roast the meat and eat it with bread made without yeast.

The blood was a sign that Israelites lived in that house and so the angel of death 'passed over' any house marked in this way.

God said that the Israelites should always celebrate that day as a special festival. Every year afterwards, they ate a 'Passover' meal, to remember how God had saved them.

Pharaoh had finally had enough. He sent for Moses and Aaron and said, "Take your people and leave at once!"

The Egyptians gave the Israelites gold and silver to try to hurry them on their way.

But after Moses and his people had left, Pharaoh changed his mind and sent his soldiers after them. They caught up with the Israelites at the Red Sea.

Moses stretched out his arms and God sent a wind to blow back the water.

The Israelites hurried across the pathway of dry land.

When the Egyptian soldiers followed, the water rushed over them and killed every one. Moses' people were free! That night, the Israelites celebrated with music and songs.

God looked after His people

EXODUS: 16-17

It did not take long for the Israelites to start grumbling. They complained that they had very little to eat. They remembered all the fish and wonderful vegetables they had had in Egypt. They forgot about their cruel masters and turned on Moses and Aaron.

"We would rather have died in Egypt, than starve to death in the desert," they moaned.

God heard their complaints. "You will have meat to eat each night and bread every day, except on the Sabbath, my day of rest," God promised.

And that night, a huge flock of birds called quail flew down and landed where the Israelites were camped. Now, there was plenty of meat for everyone.

Next morning, the ground all around the camp was covered with dew. As the dew dried, something white and flaky, as delicate as frost, was left behind.

"This is special food that God has sent for you," said Moses. "Gather as much as you need."

The Israelites collected it quickly. It tasted just like honey. It appeared each morning. And every sixth day, they collected twice as much as usual, to last them through the Sabbath, or God's day of rest. They called the food manna.

But Moses' problems did not end there. The hot sun beat down on the desert, the people's throats grew dry and they became thirstier and thirstier. There was very little water, so the grumbling began all over again.

Moses turned to God for help. "Go ahead of the people," said God, "and when you reach a rock at Mount Sinai, strike it with your stick."

Moses did as he was told. Lots of water came gushing and gurgling out from the rock, cool and refreshing – everyone had plenty to drink.

In this way, God looked after His people as they wandered through the desert on their long journey to the land of Canaan.

God's ten laws

EXODUS: 19-20, 24-27, 32, 34-40

At the foot of Mount Sinai, Moses and his people set up camp.

"I have brought you here to be my chosen people," said God. "Will you obey me?" The Israelites agreed that they would. Then, God said that He would give them ten laws, His commandments, to show them how to serve Him properly and to help them understand how to behave towards one another.

Two days later, thunder roared and lightning flashed at the top of the mountain. Moses and Aaron went up alone and there, God gave them His laws.

These are God's ten laws.

"Honour and serve Me alone, for I am the only God.

Do not make or worship any idols.

Treat My name with respect.

Keep every Sabbath as a day of rest.

Respect your father and mother.

Do not kill another human being.

Husbands and wives must keep their love only for one another.

Do not steal.

Do not tell lies.

Do not be greedy about things that other people have."

Because Moses was His special prophet, God explained to him how the laws worked. Moses explained them to the people and everyone agreed to obey the laws.

But, when Moses went back up the mountain to talk with God, he was gone so long that the people grew restless. They spoke to Aaron.

"Where has Moses gone?" they asked. "Make a new god to lead us."

Aaron collected all the gold, melted it down and made it into a golden bull calf. The people worshipped this bull.

When they saw how quickly the people had forgotten their promises, God and Moses were really angry. Moses threw the stone tablets, on which God had carved his laws, on to the ground and they smashed to pieces.

Moses was absolutely furious, but he loved his people and asked God to give them another chance. God made new stone tablets and, once more, the people kept their agreement, their 'covenant', with God.

To show that He was always near them, God asked for a special tent to be made, in which a wooden box, covered with gold, was to be kept. This box contained the stone tablets.

Everyone happily gave the things that were needed to make the tent, or tabernacle, and the finest craftsmen worked on it. It was beautiful and was lined with richly coloured linens.

Around the tent was a courtyard, where people could offer a lamb or a kid, in payment for things they had done wrong. God wanted to remind His people that He loved them. Although they were not perfect, they could always come to say they were sorry and give thanks.

In the desert for forty years

NUMBERS: 13-14, 17, 21

From Mount Sinai, the Israelites moved towards Canaan. At the border, they chose twelve men to spy out the land.

After forty days, the spies returned, carrying bunches of grapes, figs and pomegranates. "Canaan is a very fertile land," they said, "but the cities are defended like fortresses. If we try to take over the land, we will be crushed!"

The people were devastated. "We should go back to Egypt!" they cried.

Joshua and Caleb, two of the spies, protested. "No! We must trust in God. He will protect us and give us this land." But no one would listen.

God was angry. “Because you will not trust me,” He told them, “you will wander in the desert for forty years. Only Joshua and Caleb will enter Canaan.”

The Israelites didn’t like this idea and decided to fight the Canaanites, but they were very heavily defeated.

The people were angry, so they turned on Moses. "What gives you and Aaron the right to be our leaders?" they asked.

Moses replied, "Let each of our twelve tribes choose a leader and carve his name on an almond branch. Tonight, the branches will be left in God's tent. God will choose one man to lead His people."

Next morning, only Aaron's branch had burst into flower and produced almonds. He had been chosen.

Things calmed down, but when, years later, Aaron died, the complaints started again.

"Why did we leave Egypt? There's no proper food or water here. We're tired of eating manna," they moaned.

This time, God sent poisonous snakes to punish the rebels. They spread into the camp, killing people with their bites.

The Israelites pleaded with Moses. "We realise we've been wrong to speak against God. Please ask Him to take these snakes away."

So Moses prayed to God.

"Make a brass snake and fix it to a pole," said God. "Anyone who is bitten by a snake, need only look at this pole to be healed."

In this way, those who trusted God were made well again.

Down crashed the walls

JOSHUA: 1-6

Eventually, the forty years in the desert came to an end. When Moses died, God chose Joshua as the new leader.

From their camp on the far side of the River Jordan, Joshua sent two spies to Jericho.

In a house on the city wall, lived a woman called Rahab. She offered the men shelter for the night. But the king of Jericho heard of this and sent his soldiers to capture them.

Rahab hid the spies on her roof and, when questioned, told the soldiers that they had left.

Rahab knew that God intended to give Canaan to the Israelites. "We are all afraid," she said. "Promise me that you will look after my family and keep us safe when you take this city."

"We give you our word, if you promise to tell no one what we have been doing here," said the men. "When we invade, tie a red cord to the window, so we can recognise your house again. Then, gather all of your family together and we will make sure they remain safe."

And so Rahab promised. Then, she let the men down from her window on a rope and they made their way back to Joshua.

Not long afterwards, the people of Israel prepared to cross the River Jordan to take Jericho. The water in the river was very high. The priests went ahead, carrying the box with God's laws in it. As they stepped into the river, the banks collapsed upstream, damming the water. At Jericho, the people were able to cross the river bed easily.

Then, the Israelites took twelve stones from the middle of the river bed. They piled them up on to the bank, as a sign of God's help in bringing them into Canaan. Then, the river flooded through again.

The Israelites set up camp outside the walls of Jericho and celebrated Passover.

The walls of Jericho were high and thick and the gates were shut tight against the Israelites. No one could get in or out. Then, God spoke to Joshua, "Each day, for six days, you are to march round the city walls. Place seven priests at the front. The men with my box of laws must go next. The priests should have trumpets made of rams' horns and they are to blow on the horns as you march. Everyone else must be silent.

"On the seventh day, march round the city seven times. Then, the priests are to play one long note on their trumpets and all the people are to shout loudly. The walls of Jericho will fall, the city will be yours."

So each day, the Israelites went out and marched round the walls of Jericho and, each night, they returned to their camp.

On the seventh day, they marched round the city seven times. The last time, when the priests sounded the trumpets, Joshua gave the order and a great shout went up.

Down crashed the walls and the people of Israel took the city. Only Rahab and her family were saved.

The city was set on fire and burnt to the ground. This was the first of Joshua's victories in Canaan. With him as their leader, the Israelites slowly conquered the 'promised land'.

The secret of his strength

JUDGES: 13-16

Many, many years passed. But after Joshua's death, the Israelites began to forget God again. As a punishment, God let the Philistines rule over His people for forty years.

One day, God sent an angel to a man called Manoah – he was told that he and his wife would have a son, who would help protect the Israelites from their enemies.

When the boy was born, he was called Samson. As a sign that Samson belonged to God, his parents never cut his hair.

Samson grew up very strong. Once, he even killed a lion with his bare hands.

From that point, Samson realised that God had given him a special strength to use against the Philistines. And over the years, Samson did... he destroyed their crops and, once, killed a thousand of them, using only a donkey's jawbone as a weapon.

When they tried to trap him, he always escaped.

The Philistines were determined to have their revenge.

Their chance came when Samson fell in love with a beautiful Philistine girl, called Delilah. The five Philistine kings went to her. "We will each give you eleven hundred silver coins, if you can make Samson tell you the secret of his strength," they said. Delilah agreed.

But, each time Delilah asked Samson to tell her the secret of his strength, he told a different story. "If you tie me up with new bowstrings, I'll be as weak as anybody else," he said and then, "use brand new rope to tie me up… weave my hair into a loom… "

Delilah tried all these but, Samson remained strong. "If you won't tell me, you don't really love me," Delilah nagged.

Eventually, Samson gave in. "My hair is a sign that I belong to God. If it were cut, I would lose all my strength," he told her.

So, that night, when Samson was fast asleep, Delilah called a man to cut off his hair. Then, the Philistines came and took him prisoner.

Samson was blinded, chained and taken to a prison in Gaza and made to work very hard.

But slowly, Samson's hair grew back.

One day, the Philistines held a feast in honour of their god, Dagon. They had Samson brought from the prison to the temple. The place was crowded with thousands of people, who jeered and laughed at him.

Samson prayed to God to give him strength. He reached out and pushed with all his might against the two pillars that supported the building. The temple collapsed and all inside were killed. It was Samson's final act against the enemies of Israel. He had been leader for twenty years.

Your God will be my God

RUTH: 1-4

Many years later, there was a famine in Israel. One man from Bethlehem took his wife, Naomi, and his two sons to live in Moab.

Sadly, it wasn't long before the father died. The sons grew up and married but, ten years later, both men also died.

Naomi, feeling all alone, decided it was time to return to her homeland. Her daughters-in-law, Orpah and Ruth, set out with her. "You must go back to your people," Naomi told them.

Unhappily, Orpah agreed, but Ruth said, "I'm coming with you. Your people will be my people, your God will be my God."

Eventually, Naomi and Ruth reached the town of Bethlehem at harvest time. They were very poor so, every day, Ruth walked behind the workers in the fields, collecting any corn that had been dropped. She then exchanged the corn for a small amount of money. The hours were long and it was very hard work.

Unknown to her, she had chosen the field of one of Naomi's relatives, a rich man called Boaz. When he came to check the work, he noticed Ruth and asked about her. Hearing that she was a relative of Naomi's, he told her that she was always welcome to work in his field.

Naomi was delighted when Ruth told her. She wanted to find a husband for Ruth and she knew that Boaz was a good man. In Israel at that time, the nearest relative would take care of a man's family if he died. Naomi wanted to claim this right, so she sent Ruth to find out if he would marry her.

Boaz agreed, which made Naomi very happy and, eventually, Ruth and he had a son.

So it was that Ruth, who had put her trust in the God of Israel and had helped and loved her mother-in-law, was to become the great-grandmother of Israel's greatest king – David.

We want a king

1 SAMUEL: 1, 8-10, 15-16

Near Jerusalem, there lived a woman called Hannah. She had no children and this made her very sad. One day, when Hannah was praying silently to God, she didn't realise she was mouthing the words to her prayer.

Eli, the priest, watched her and, seeing her lips move without the words being spoken, he believed she was drunk. When Hannah explained, Eli said, “May God give you the son you long for.”

In time, God did give Hannah a son – Samuel. When he was old enough, Hannah took the boy back to Eli. “This is the son God gave me,” she said. “Now I am giving him back to God.”

So Samuel grew up loving and obeying God.

In time, God chose Samuel to lead the Israelites. Samuel was a good and gentle man, who loved God and the simple, honest way of life of his people. His two sons, however, were not like him. They were only interested in money. The Israelites did not want either of them to lead when Samuel died, so they asked Samuel for a king to rule over them, as in other nations.

Samuel was worried. God was the only true leader, so he prayed for guidance.

God told Samuel to tell the people what a king would be like. "He will make your sons fight in his armies," said Samuel. "He will force you to work the land for him and he will take the best crops. You will become his slaves."

But the people insisted.

When Samuel told God that his words hadn't changed the Israelites' minds, God replied, "Do as they wish. Give them their king."

One day, Samuel met a tall, handsome man – Saul. God had told Samuel where and when he would meet Israel's future king and so was not surprised when he heard God say, "This is the man who is to rule."

At dawn the next day, following tradition, Samuel poured oil onto Saul's head, as a sign that he was the chosen one.

At first, Saul was a good and popular king. Under his leadership, his people won many battles, but soon, he became proud. He began to think more of himself than he did of God. So, God told Samuel that it was time to find a new king.

God told Samuel to go to Bethlehem, as He had chosen one of Jesse's sons to succeed Saul.

When Samuel arrived, he invited Jesse and his sons to witness an offering for God. He spoke to all of the sons in turn. Each time, he thought, "This fine-looking, young man must be the chosen one." But each time, God said, "No."

"What's important is not what a person looks like," God said, "but what he is like inside."

After Samuel had rejected seven of Jesse's sons, he asked if there were any more. Jesse said that the youngest, David, was out looking after the sheep. Samuel asked Jesse to send for him.

As David walked in, God spoke to Samuel, saying, "This is the one!"

So, Samuel anointed David and from that time on, David always felt that God was with him.

The champion of Israel

1 SAMUEL: 16-17

David continued looking after his father's sheep. Each day, he grew in wisdom and strength. He had to be skillful and strong to fight off the wild animals, that often attacked the flock. David began to use a sling shot, to scare off the bears and lions and soon became an expert with it.

To while away the time, David also practised playing his harp and he quickly became very good at this, too. News of his skills spread far across the land.

Meanwhile, Samuel no longer visited Saul at his palace and the king felt distant from God. He had terrible moods and was tormented by an evil spirit.

One of Saul's attendants suggested that harp music might soothe the king.

David was sent for and indeed, whenever David played, the music calmed Saul. Once the king felt better, David would return home.

Then, news came that the Philistines had set up camp on one side of the Valley of Elah. Only a small stream separated them from the Israelite army, who were on the other side.

The Philistines had a mighty champion in their army – Goliath – nearly three metres tall and stronger than an ox. He paraded up and down, day after day, jeering at the Israelites.

"Where's the champion of Israel?" he would shout. "Send him to fight me! If he kills me, we will be your slaves. If I kill him, you will be ours." But no one would face Goliath. They were all too terrified.

David had three brothers in Saul's army. One day, when he was bringing food to them, he heard Goliath's taunts across the valley.

"Who is he, to challenge the army of the living God?" David said. "Let me go and fight him."

The soldiers looked at the boy and laughed. But, when Saul heard about this, he sent for David.

“I’ve fought lions and bears to protect my father’s sheep,” David told him. “God protected me then and He will do so now.”

Saul eventually agreed. He gave David his own armour and his sword. But because the armour was so heavy and large, David couldn’t move with it on. So, he took it all off and picked up his sling. He chose five smooth stones from the stream and went out to meet the giant.

When Goliath saw him coming, he roared with laughter. "Is this your champion?" he sneered at the Israelites.

"I come in the name of the God of Israel," said David, calmly. "He will put you in my power."

He took a stone from his bag, placed it into his sling and took aim. The stone hurtled towards Goliath and struck him on the forehead with such force, that it broke his skull. The giant man fell face down on the ground.

When the Philistines saw that their hero was dead, they ran into the hills. The joyful Israelites gave chase – victory and the land of the Philistines was theirs!

A great leader

2 SAMUEL: 1-6, 11-19; 1 KINGS: 1

Years later, after Saul's death, David became King of Israel, but there were difficult times ahead for him. Supporters of Saul fought against David and the Philistines were always waiting for a chance to return to the country. David longed to conquer the city of Jerusalem, so that he could bring the sacred box of God's laws there.

What a celebration they had when, at last, David attacked and captured the city! There was music and dancing, feasts were held and gifts were offered – David had made Jerusalem the city of God.

David was a great leader, loved by all his people and faithful to God. But he was not perfect. He fell in love with Bathsheba, even though she was already married. David made sure that her soldier husband was killed in a battle. God saw what David had done and let him know through Nathan, the prophet. David prayed to God to forgive him and God saw that he was truly sorry.

"You will remain King," God said to David, "but the task of building my temple I will give to your son, Solomon."

Alone and upset, King David began to draw up plans for the temple and wrote music that would be used there to praise God.

Later, David married Bathsheba and his kingdom remained strong, although trouble was rarely far away.

Absalom, one of David's sons, was handsome and popular – and he wanted to be king. So, he plotted to take his father's throne and marched on Jerusalem.

At first, King David took flight, but then he rallied his army and went into battle against his son. David's army defeated Absalom, who tried to flee, but was captured by some of David's soldiers. They ignored the King's orders to spare Absalom's life and killed him.

The King was overcome with grief.

"Oh, my son, my son," he cried, "I wish that I had died in your place!"

As Absalom was dead, David's next son, Adonijah, decided that he would claim the throne for himself. But King David said that Solomon would succeed him.

David told Zadok the priest, Nathan the prophet and Benaiah to take Solomon to Gihon, to anoint him as king.

The wisest of men

1 KINGS: 1-4, 10

There was great celebration when Solomon became king.

Before he died, King David spoke to Solomon. "Be a strong king. Trust in God and follow His commands. Then God will keep His promise that my descendants will rule this nation."

Immediately, King Solomon expelled his father's old enemies and set out new districts throughout his kingdom.

Solomon ruled over
the kingdom of Israel for
many years and loved God.
He was to become one of Israel's
most famous kings. And the people
of God lived together in a time of peace.

One night, God appeared before Solomon in a dream. "What would you like me to give you?" God asked.

"I am very young to rule over so many people," Solomon replied. "Please give me the wisdom I need to make the right and true decisions."

God was very pleased, because Solomon had not asked for things for himself.

"I'll give you more wisdom and understanding," said God, "than anyone has ever had before."

God kept his promise and Solomon became the wisest of men. But Solomon always remembered that his wisdom came from God.

One day, Solomon had to judge who was the real mother of a baby. Solomon thought and then suggested that they cut the baby in half. The false mother agreed. But the real mother said, "No!" The wise king knew at once who the real mother was.

Such tales of Solomon's wisdom spread far and wide across the world. Eventually, they reached the land of Sheba.

When the queen of that land heard about Solomon, she decided to see for herself how wise Solomon was.

She thought up a list of very difficult questions and then, taking jewels, gold and spices with her, set out for Jerusalem. She made quite an impression when she entered the city!

The queen asked Solomon all her questions and he was able to answer them all easily. "I can see," she said, "that God has given His people a wise king, because He loves them so much."

A wonderful temple for God

1 KINGS: 5-8

In the fourth year of Solomon's reign, he began to build a wonderful temple for God.

For the foundations and walls, fine large stones were used, as well as quality woods, such as cedar.

Because lots of cedar wood was needed and the best cedars grew in Tyre, Solomon made a treaty with Hiram, the king of that country.

Once cut, the wood was tied together in rafts and floated down the coast, to where Solomon was building the temple. In return, Solomon supplied Tyre with loads of wheat and olive oil.

The temple was going to be a wonderful place where God's special box, containing the laws, would be kept.

When the temple was finished, it was amazing. At the rear was a windowless square, with floors and walls covered in gold. The room would hold the box containing God's laws. It was decorated with carved figures of winged creatures, palm trees and flowers, also covered in gold.

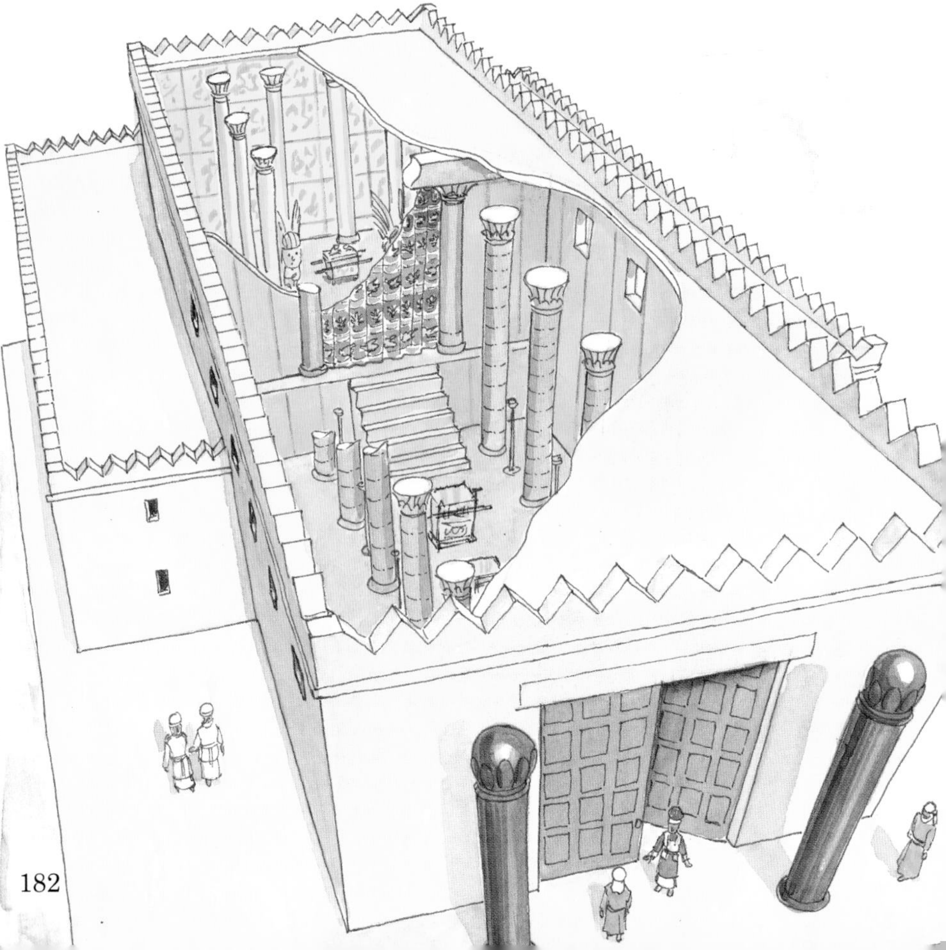

The outer room had a gold altar and ten gold lamp stands. The other furnishings in the temple were made of gold, including the tables, cups, bowls and even the pans that were used to carry coal to the fires. It was as beautiful as King Solomon could make it and contained the very best of everything.

Outside were courtyards, where people could offer their gifts to God.

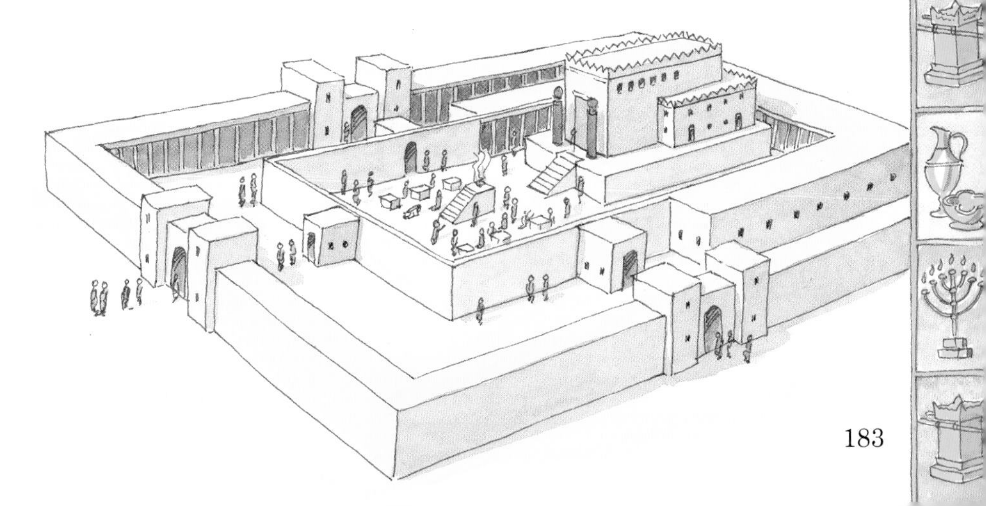

Thousands of men had worked on the temple and it had taken seven years to complete.

So, Solomon decided to hold a very special ceremony. The priests made offerings and the box containing God's laws was carried inside. It was then that the temple was completely filled with a dazzling light – the presence of God. King Solomon prayed, "Lord, God of Israel, hear the prayers of your people. Listen to them in your home in heaven and help them always."

Then, Solomon spoke to his people, "Be true to God and obey His commands."

After the ceremony, a great feast was held and the celebrations lasted for a week.

Israel will be taken

1 KINGS: 11

During Solomon's reign, Israel flourished. Beautiful buildings and great cities were built. But, to pay for the buildings, people had to pay taxes. Men had to work for the king and not on their own farms.

Solomon also married many foreign princesses, who worshipped their own gods. It helped to keep peace between the lands and it was good for trade, but it also brought many problems.

Over many years, Solomon was persuaded by his wives to worship these foreign gods. He did not remain faithful to God, as his father had.

So, God said to him, “The kingdom of Israel will be taken from your son, since you have not followed my commands.”

Eventually, this came to pass.

The true God

1 KINGS: 12, 16-19

After Solomon's death, Israel was divided in two. The southern part, Judah, followed Solomon's son – Rehoboam. In the north, the people followed Jeroboam, son of Nebat.

None of the kings, who succeeded Jeroboam, were faithful to God. One king, Ahab, married a woman called Jezebel and began to worship her god, Baal. Queen Jezebel had many of the prophets, who remained loyal to God, killed. But one prophet, Elijah, spoke out for the Lord.

One day, Elijah brought a message to King Ahab – there would be no rain in Israel until God said so.

After Elijah had delivered the message, God told him to go to a place on the other side of the River Jordan, where he would be safe.

For three years, Elijah stayed away and God watched over him, sending ravens to bring him food and telling Elijah where to find people who would look after him.

And in all that time, it did not rain once.

One day, God told Elijah to return to Ahab.

"Why have you come back, troublemaker?" asked the King.

"You have disobeyed God," replied Elijah. "Send your people and the prophets of Baal to meet me on Mount Carmel."

Ahab did as Elijah had asked and when everyone was gathered together, Elijah said, "It is time to see who is the true God."

Then, Elijah challenged the prophets of Baal.

"Offer a bull to Baal and I will offer one to God. The true God will be the one who sends fire from the sky and sets light to the altar."

The priests of Baal made their altar and laid a bull on it. They called out to their god all day, but there was silence and nothing happened.

Elijah built his altar with a ditch surrounding it, which he filled with water. He placed his bull on the wood and poured water over everything. Then, Elijah began to pray. God sent fire down and, even though the wood was soaked, it burst into flames.

The people cried, "The Lord is the true God."

Then, Elijah asked God for rain. The skies grew dark and a strong wind blew and the rain fell once more. It was a wonderful day for Elijah. But Queen Jezebel swore to kill the prophet, in revenge for what he had done.

Elijah heard about the queen's plan and fled.

He travelled a great distance and arrived, at last, at Mount Sinai. Suddenly, he heard God's voice, asking why he was there.

"The people of Israel have killed all your prophets. I am the only one left," Elijah explained. "Now they want to kill me."

"You must go back," God replied. "There is lots more work to be done."

The prophet Isaiah

ISAIAH: 9, 11

More than a hundred years after Elijah's death, the northern part of Israel fell to the Assyrians and the people were taken into exile.

The southern kingdom of Judah was also under threat from Assyria, but God sent the prophet Isaiah to help King Hezekiah to save Jerusalem. The city was safe for a time, but Isaiah warned the King, "You must remember, Jerusalem will not fall, if you obey God's laws."

Isaiah also gave the people a lasting message of hope. "For unto us a child is born, a son is given and government will be on his shoulders," said Isaiah. "He will be called the Mighty God, Everlasting Father, Prince of Peace. There will be no end to his rule and peace."

Everything Isaiah said came true.

Thrown to the lions

DANIEL: 1, 6

Over many, many years, God's people continued to disobey Him. So, the Lord allowed the king of Babylon, Nebuchadnezzar, to gain control of Judah.

The king took many people as prisoners, including a group of young boys from Jerusalem, one of whom was Daniel.

Then, the king ordered his chief official to pick men from noble families, who could be trained to serve in the royal court. Daniel and his friends were some of the chosen men.

As they grew up, they studied the great writings and learnt to speak Babylonian. As the years passed, Daniel became very wise.

Then, one year, the Persians captured Babylon and their leader, Darius, became king.

Darius made Daniel one of his chief advisors and Daniel served him loyally. But the king's other advisors grew jealous of Daniel and the attention he received and plotted against him.

When they discovered that he prayed to God everyday, they said, "If we want to get Daniel into trouble, it will have to be something to do with his religion."

The advisors persuaded the king to make a new law, saying that for thirty days, no one was to ask for anything from any god or any human being, except from the king himself. Anyone who broke the law was to be thrown to the lions.

Daniel heard about the law, but continued to pray three times a day. He made no secret of it. His enemies were delighted – their plan had worked and they rushed to tell the king.

What could the king do? Daniel had broken the law. The king was very upset. He liked Daniel, but could not find a way to save him.

So, at sunset, Daniel was thrown into a deep pit, filled with hungry lions.

That night, the king couldn't eat.

He didn't want music.

He couldn't sleep.

He paced up and down.

As soon as dawn broke, Darius hurried off to the lion pit.

The king didn't expect to find Daniel alive and called down to the pit, "Was your God able to save you from the lions?"

Darius expected silence. But, instead, he heard Daniel's reply, "Yes, Your Majesty. God knew that I was innocent and He has kept me safe. I have done you no wrong."

Darius was amazed. He gave orders to have Daniel set free and for the men who accused him to be thrown to the lions instead.

The king made a new law. "Let everyone in my kingdom fear and respect the God of Daniel, for He is the one true, living God."

An enormous fish

JONAH: 1-4

Being God's messenger was often a dangerous and unpopular job and not all of the prophets were willing to say "Yes" to God's call to them. One reluctant prophet was Jonah.

One day, God told Jonah that he was to go to the city of Nineveh, the capital of Assyria. The Assyrians were the enemies of God's people.

"Tell the Assyrians, in forty days, Nineveh will be destroyed," said God. "I know about the wicked things they are doing – they must stop!"

"I am going to look stupid," Jonah thought to himself. "God is loving and forgives people. He will not destroy Nineveh."

So, Jonah went to Joppa instead and boarded a boat that was bound for Spain.

God was angry with Jonah for not doing what He had asked. No sooner had the boat set sail, than God created a huge storm. Everyone feared that the boat would be ripped apart.

"Pray to your gods," the crew shouted.

Meanwhile, Jonah was fast asleep below deck. When the captain woke him and told him to pray like everyone else, Jonah wouldn't.

The storm worsened and, as the boat was tossed about, Jonah told the crew, "It's my fault that you are caught in this violent storm. Throw me into the sea and it will calm down."

The captain refused but, as the storm got worse, he had no choice and reluctantly threw Jonah overboard. The sea instantly calmed.

Jonah was convinced that he would drown and, as he sank down into the ocean, he called out for help.

God heard his cries and sent an enormous fish, that swallowed him alive.

For three days, Jonah was inside the dark belly of the huge fish. He was truly sorry for disobeying God and told Him in his prayers.

God listened to Jonah and, when He was sure that Jonah was truly sorry, He made the fish throw Jonah up onto a beach.

Once again, God told Jonah to take his message to Nineveh. Jonah rushed off at once.

The people of Nineveh listened to Jonah and immediately changed how they lived. God saw that they had given up their wicked ways and did not destroy the city.

"This is exactly what I said you would do!" Jonah complained to God. "So now, let me die." He sat outside the city, in the scorching sun.

But, God made a plant grow up to shade Jonah and he began to feel less miserable.

Next day, the plant died and the sun beat down again.

“I’m sorry that the plant has gone. I was glad of it,” said Jonah.

“You did not make that plant grow, but you are sorry for it,” said God. “Just think how I feel about the people of Nineveh – the innocent children, the animals – I gave them all life.”

At last, Jonah understood how much God still loved and cared for His world.

The King of Peace

MICAH: 5

There were many times when the people of Israel forgot God's laws and many times when His prophets warned of the trouble this would bring. Some prophets also spoke of the wonderful things God planned for the future.

The prophet Micah spoke of God's promise of a ruler for Israel, who would come from the tiny town of Bethlehem.

"He will rule over his people with the majesty of God," said Micah. "And it won't be in just Israel that he is famous. All over the world, people will recognise his greatness. He will be the King of Peace."

Micah was speaking about Jesus, whose story is told in The New Testament.

THE NEW TESTAMENT

The angel messenger

LUKE: 1

In Nazareth, a small town in Galilee, to the north of Israel, there lived a girl named Mary. She was engaged to Joseph, who was a descendant of King David. Joseph was the town carpenter.

One day, as Mary went about her daily tasks, she noticed a stranger watching her.

"I am Gabriel," the stranger told her. "Peace be with you, Mary. The Lord God has sent me with a special message for you. He has greatly blessed you."

Mary stared at the angel messenger.
She wondered what he could have to tell her.

Gabriel could see that Mary was frightened.

"Do not be afraid, Mary," he said. "God loves you very much. He has chosen you, above all others, to be the mother of his promised King. You will have a baby, God's own son. You will name him Jesus."

But Mary did not understand.

"How can this be?" she asked.

"The Holy Spirit will fall upon you and God's power will rest within you. He will take care of everything," Gabriel told Mary. "Remember your cousin, Elizabeth, who thought she could never have children? She is expecting a baby, too. God can do anything, if you trust Him."

Then, Mary knew that she did not need to ask any more questions. She just needed to trust in God.

"I am the Lord's servant," she said. "I will do whatever He wants."

Chosen

MATTHEW: 1

When Joseph found that Mary was expecting a baby, he was greatly troubled. Joseph was a good man and did not want to disgrace Mary in public. So, he decided to quietly break off their engagement.

Before he did so, Joseph had a dream, in which an angel of the Lord spoke to him. "Do not break your engagement to Mary," he told Joseph. "She has done nothing wrong. She has been chosen to be the mother of God's son and you will name the baby Jesus. He will grow up to save the world from its' sins."

When Joseph woke up, he knew what he must do. He would marry Mary and look after the baby, as the angel had told him to do.

The little town of Bethlehem

LUKE: 2

Not long afterwards, an order was sent out across the Roman Empire by the Emperor Augustus. He wanted to make sure that all the people were paying their taxes.

The only way to do this was by making everyone return to the town where their family came from, so that their names could be written down and recorded.

Because Joseph's family came from a town called Bethlehem, in Judea, he and Mary had no choice, but to return there. They set out on the long journey, with Mary sitting on their donkey.

Mary's baby was due to be born at any moment and she was exhausted. After travelling for many days and nights, they finally reached the little town of Bethlehem.

The town was noisy and overcrowded with all the people who had come to register. Mary and Joseph searched for somewhere to stay.

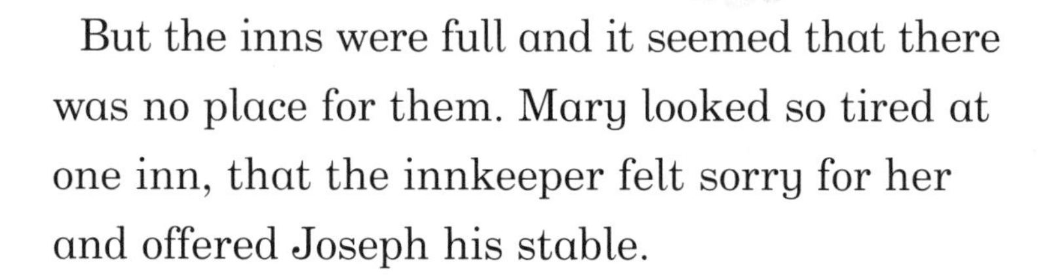

But the inns were full and it seemed that there was no place for them. Mary looked so tired at one inn, that the innkeeper felt sorry for her and offered Joseph his stable.

The stable was full of animals and very smelly and dirty, but at least it was somewhere for Mary to rest.

Mary gave birth to her son that very night. She wrapped him warmly, in strips of cloth and laid him gently in a manger, to sleep.

The shepherds

LUKE: 2

Out on the hills above Bethlehem, shepherds were looking after their flocks of sheep.

Suddenly, there was a dazzling blaze of light in the sky above them. The shepherds were terrified. They had to cover their eyes. Whatever could it be?

Then, the angel of the Lord appeared and spoke to the shepherds.

“Do not be afraid,” said the angel. “I come with good news, which will bring great joy to all people. God’s promised King, your Saviour, has been born in Bethlehem today. Go now and look for the baby. You will find him asleep, lying in a manger.”

Then, a huge crowd of angels appeared in the sky, singing, “Praise be to God. Peace to everyone on earth.”

The angels disappeared and the sky went dark again. The shepherds knew they had to hurry to Bethlehem, to see this new baby. They made their sheep safe and set off.

In Bethlehem, they found Mary and Joseph, with their baby. He was asleep in a manger, just as the angel had said.

The shepherds told Mary and Joseph all the things the angel had told them. Then, they set off for the fields again. As they made their way back to their sheep, they sang songs praising God. They would never forget this night.

The three wise men

MATTHEW: 2

Far away to the east, some wise men, who studied the skies, had noticed a special star. They knew it was an important sign and decided to follow it, to see where it led. They travelled many days and nights and eventually arrived in Jerusalem.

"Where is the baby, who is born to be King of the Jews?" they asked. "We have seen his star and we have come to worship him."

When Herod, who already was the King of the Jews, heard about the wise men, he was furious.

He called together all of his chief priests and advisors and asked them where this new king could be found.

"In the town of Bethlehem in Judea," they replied. "That is what God's prophets wrote."

So, Herod arranged a secret meeting with the three wise men. He wanted to know the exact time that the star had appeared, so that he could work out how old the baby was. Then, he sent them on to Bethlehem to find the baby. He pretended that he, too, wanted to see the baby and pay his respects. But he had something much more evil in mind!

The wise men left Jerusalem and were overjoyed to see ahead of them the star they had noticed in the east.

When it stopped over one of the houses in Bethlehem, they knew that they had finally found their King.

Inside the house, where Mary and Joseph were now staying, the three wise men knelt before the baby Jesus and gave him the presents they had brought – gold, sweet-smelling frankincense and a spicy-smelling ointment, called myrrh.

Not long afterwards, in a dream, God warned the wise men not to go back to Herod, but to journey home by another road.

When they left, God sent a messenger to warn Joseph, too.

"Herod will be looking for the child, in order to kill him. You must take him and Mary to Egypt, at once. Stay there, until I tell you it is safe to leave."

So, Joseph and Mary gathered their things together and fled towards Egypt.

My Father's house

LUKE: 2

After Herod's death, God's messenger told Mary and Joseph to return to their home in Galilee. So, Jesus grew up in Nazareth and was a very keen student.

When he was twelve years old, his parents took him to Jerusalem to celebrate the Feast of the Passover.

On the way back home, Mary and Joseph thought Jesus was travelling somewhere in their large family group and did not worry that they had not seen him for a while.

They journeyed for a whole day, before they realised that Jesus was missing. They started to look for him amongst their family and friends, but no one had seen him.

That night, they lay awake, unable to sleep for fear and worry.

Early next morning, they returned to Jerusalem and searched the whole city for him.

On the third day, they found him in the temple. He was sitting with the men who taught God's Laws, carefully listening to everything they had to say, as well as asking questions himself. Everyone who heard him was amazed at how much of the teachings he understood.

"Why have you worried us like this?" Mary asked him. "You must have known, Jesus, how anxious we would be."

Jesus seemed surprised.

"Surely you knew that I would be here, in my Father's house?" he said.

Joseph and Mary did not understand what Jesus meant and Jesus did not explain further. Then, they all journeyed back to Nazareth.

God's King is coming

MATTHEW: 3; MARK: 1; LUKE: 3; JOHN: 1

Mary's cousin, Elizabeth, had given birth to a son, called John and his father, Zechariah, brought him up to follow God's Laws.

When he was older, John went to live alone in the desert of Judea. He wore clothes of camel hair and ate locusts and wild honey. John was God's messenger and people came from Judea, Jerusalem and far and wide to hear him speak.

"God's King is coming soon," he would tell them. "Say sorry to God. Change your ways and be baptised, then God will forgive you the things that you have done wrong."

John took all those who wanted God's forgiveness to the banks of the River Jordan. He led them in and dipped their heads below the water. This was called 'baptism'. It was a sign that God had forgiven them their sins and had washed them away.

John taught people that they should share what they had with those less fortunate than themselves. Some of them began to wonder if he could be the promised King.

But John said, "I am here to tell you that someone much greater than I will come soon and I am not worthy to carry his shoes."

At this time, Jesus arrived from Nazareth and came to the River Jordan to be baptised by John. They had never met before, but John knew at once, that this was God's promised King.

"You should be baptising me, Lord," said John.

But Jesus persuaded him.

Then, as Jesus came up out of the water, God's spirit came down upon him in the form of a dove and a voice came from Heaven, saying, "This is my own blessed Son and I am pleased with him."

Changed into wine

MARK 1; JOHN 2

Soon afterwards, John was put into prison. So, Jesus went about Galilee preaching the same message, “The Kingdom of God is near. Change your ways and believe the good news!”

Along the way, he met people who were to become his followers, including Andrew and his brother, Simon (whom Jesus called Peter), John and Nathaneal.

One day, as he travelled through the country, Jesus was invited to a wedding in Cana, along with his mother and his friends. During the wedding feast, the wine ran out and Mary told Jesus of this. Nervously, Jesus began to speak, “It is not yet my time... ” But Mary had already turned away to the servants and said, “Do exactly what he tells you to do.”

Nearby stood six large water-jars. Guests had used the water from them to wash with before the meal, according to Jewish law. Now, the water-jars stood empty.

"Fill these jars with water," said Jesus, to the servants. "Then, pour out a little of the water and take it to the man in charge of the meal."

The servants did as they were told and took the water to the man.

It had changed into wine!

The man in charge called to the bridegroom.

"Everyone else serves the best wine first and keeps the ordinary wine until last. But you have saved the best until now!"

This was the first of the miracles that Jesus performed and only the servants who had drawn the water knew Jesus' secret.

Chosen twelve

MATTHEW: 4, 10; MARK: 1, 3; LUKE: 5, 6

News about Jesus and his teachings quickly spread. He spoke with such authority and power, that crowds of people came from all around to hear him speak.

One day, Jesus was preaching on the shores of Lake Gennesaret. The crowd got bigger and bigger and began to push closer and closer to the shore. Jesus noticed two fishing boats pulled up onto the beach. The fishermen were nearby, washing their nets. Jesus stepped into one of the boats and asked Simon, the fisherman, to take him a little way out onto the lake. And from there, sitting in the boat, he was able to continue teaching the people.

When he had finished, Jesus told Simon to row further out and drop his fishing nets into the lake.

"We have worked all night, without any luck," Simon said. "But, if you say so, we will try again."

Simon and his brother, Andrew, took the boat out further and let the nets down into the water. Immediately, they filled with such a huge number of fish that the nets almost broke and the boat started to sink!

“Come, help us!” the two men shouted to James and John, who were in the other boat. The fishermen were astonished.

As the boats reached the shore again, loaded with their catch, Jesus said, “Do not be afraid. I want you all to follow me. From now on, you will be catchers of people, not fish.”

So, the four men left their boats on the shore and became followers of Jesus.

One day, Jesus went to see a tax collector, called Levi and told him to leave everything behind and follow him. So, Levi got straight up and did just that!

Tax collectors were not popular with the Jewish people, as they collected taxes for the Romans. Many made extra money by over-charging the Jews. So, when Levi gave a feast for Jesus at his house, some of the more religious people were disgusted that Jesus went.

"Why do you eat and drink with such outcasts, Jesus?" they demanded, angrily.

"People who are well do not need a doctor," replied Jesus. "Like a doctor, I heal the sick. I do not need to help those who have already *found* God. I have come to help those who are *far away* from God."

On some nights, when Jesus had finished teaching and the crowds had gone home, he often went up into the hills, where he could be quiet and pray. Sometimes, he prayed all night.

Once, Jesus called his followers together. He had chosen twelve of the most loyal to be his special friends or disciples. These twelve were: Simon (whom Jesus named Peter) and his brother Andrew, James and John, Philip and Bartholomew, Matthew, Thomas, James (son of Alphaeus), Simon, Judas (son of James) and Judas Iscariot.

Jesus explained to them why God had sent him to earth. The disciples became his closest friends and travelled with him wherever he went, witnessing the wonderful things that he did.

The paralysed man

MATTHEW: 9; MARK: 2; LUKE: 5

News spread across the land that Jesus could cure people who were sick and diseased. Soon, crowds came from far and wide, just to be touched by him.

One day, Jesus was teaching at a house. So many people arrived to hear him, that the house quickly filled up. There was no room left anywhere. Even outside, people waited in crowds just to see and touch Jesus.

Then, four men arrived. They were carrying a friend on his bedmat. The poor man was paralysed and the friends truly believed that Jesus would be able to cure him. But, try as they might, they could not find a way through the crowd and into the house to see Jesus.

The men did not give up. Instead, they carried their friend up onto the flat roof, made a hole and lowered the paralysed man down to where Jesus was speaking and teaching.

When Jesus saw what the men had done, he was moved by their faith. How caring they were, to do so much for their friend. Jesus turned to the man on the mat and said, "Your sins are forgiven."

There were also some teachers of the Law in the house and they were furious that Jesus would dare to say this.

"How can he talk like this?" they thought. "Only God Himself can forgive sins."

Jesus knew exactly what the teachers were thinking.

"Why do you feel like that?" he asked. "Tell me, which do you think it is easier to do – to say to this man, 'Your sins are forgiven', or to make him get up and walk again? I want you to understand that God has given the Son of Man the power to do both these things."

Then, Jesus spoke to the man on the mat. "Get up, pick up your mat and go home!"

As they watched, the man did as Jesus said. Everyone was amazed. and praised God, saying, "We have never seen anything like this before."

Our Father in heaven

MATTHEW: 5-7; LUKE: 6

Jesus often went up into the hills around Galilee. One day, a crowd gathered to hear him speak to them about blessings from God.

"Happy are the poor in spirit, for theirs is the Kingdom of heaven," said Jesus. "God will comfort everyone who mourns and reward those who are humble.

"Happy are they who want to do God's desire, for they shall be fulfilled. Show mercy to others and mercy will be shown to you. The pure in heart shall see God and those who work for peace will be called God's children. If you are ill-treated for doing what He asks, the Kingdom of heaven will belong to you. Be happy, for great is your reward in heaven."

Jesus used everyday pictures to help the people understand his teachings more easily.

"You are like the salt we put in our food to stop it rotting. You will keep God's world from going bad," he said.

"Your kind deeds will be like lamps shining out in the darkness, lighting up God's world. People will thank God for them.

"God has given you Laws and you must follow them in all ways. God says, 'You shall not murder anyone.' But it is also wrong to feel angry enough to *want* to murder someone. God wants us to love our enemies and to show kindness to those who do us wrong."

Then, Jesus spoke to them about prayer.

"Go somewhere quiet when you want to pray and speak to God. He knows exactly what you need. This is how you should pray to Him:

Our Father in heaven,
May Your holy name be honoured;
May Your kingdom come;
May Your will be done on earth,
as it is in heaven.
Give us today, the food we need.
Forgive us the wrongs we have done,
As we forgive the wrongs that others
have done to us.
Do not bring us to the point of temptation,
But keep us safe from evil.

Ask and trust God," Jesus said, "and He will not let you down.

"Do not store up money or buy things here on earth that could be taken from you. Instead, store up your riches in heaven, where God will give you everything you need," said Jesus.

"Do not worry where your next meal will come from. Look around you, at the birds in the air...

"… they do not sow seeds or gather a harvest, but God takes care of them. You are far more important to Him than they are.

"Do not worry about what you are going to wear. Look at the way God has clothed the flowers in the fields. They do not work, but He takes care of them all the same. Put your trust in God and He will provide you with all these things."

Good, solid foundations

MATTHEW: 7

People loved to listen to Jesus telling them stories. "If you follow my teachings," he said, "you will be like a person building a house on good, solid foundations, like in this story...

"Two men decided to build houses for themselves. The wise man built his house on rock. The rains came, the floods rose and the winds blew, but his house stood firm.

"But, if you ignore what I say, you are like the other man. He was foolish enough to build his house on sand. There were no foundations and, when the rains, floods and winds came, his house fell down!"

Everyone who listened to Jesus' stories was amazed at how simply they told the truth of God.

A Roman officer

MATTHEW: 8; LUKE: 7

Once, when Jesus had finished talking, he went to a town called Capernaum, where there lived a Roman officer.

Generally, the Jews hated the Roman soldiers, but this particular Roman was very different. He was kind to the local people.

One day, his servant fell ill. When the officer heard that Jesus was in town, he asked his Jewish friends if they would go to Jesus, to see if he would come and heal the man.

"Please come," the friends begged Jesus. "This Roman officer really deserves your help. He is a good man. He paid for a synagogue to be built for us."

So, Jesus agreed and set off towards the soldier's house with them.

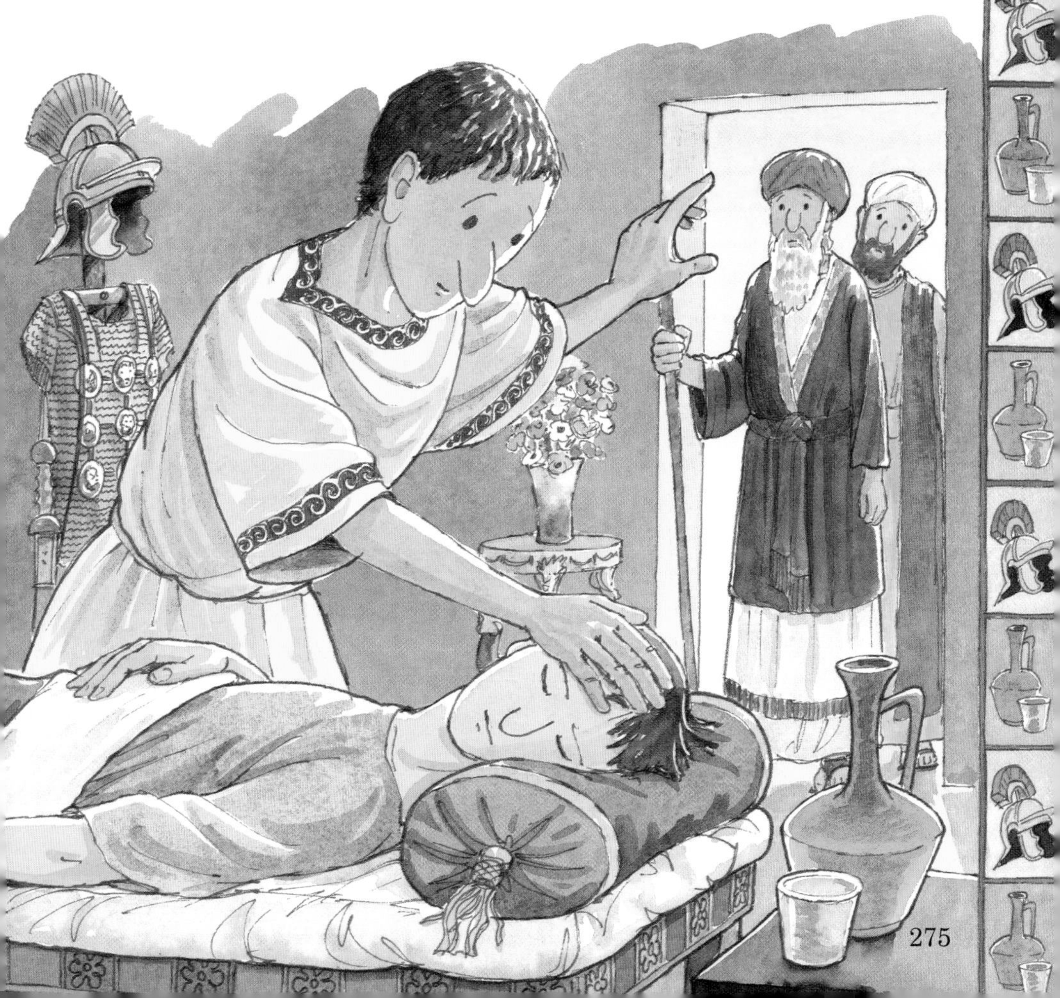

They had almost reached the house, when some more friends of the officer arrived.

The Roman had asked his friends to tell Jesus not to come into his house. He felt that he was not good enough for Jesus to enter, or good enough to bring the message to Jesus in person. He said that he knew his servant would get better if Jesus gave the order, like a soldier.

Jesus was amazed. He turned and spoke to the crowd that was following him.

"I have never seen faith like this," he said, "not even among the Jews." Then, he sent this message back to the officer, "As you have believed in me, it shall be done."

When the messengers returned to the officer's house, they found that the servant was well again, just as Jesus had promised.

A fierce storm

MATTHEW: 8; MARK: 4; LUKE: 8

One evening, when Jesus had finished his teachings, he suggested to his followers that they get into a boat and cross to the other side of the lake.

So, off they set and, with the gentle water lapping against the boat's side, it was not long before Jesus fell fast asleep. It had been a long day and he was very tired.

After a while, the wind suddenly changed. It grew much stronger and whipped the water up into huge waves. A fierce storm blew up. The waves grew bigger and bigger and washed over the sides of the little boat. But all the noise and commotion did not wake Jesus.

Some of Jesus' followers were fishermen and had seen many storms before. But, even these men began to be afraid. How was it possible for Jesus to go on sleeping, in such bad weather? They shook him awake.

"Master, wake up!" they shouted. "We are all going to die."

Jesus stood up. "Be still!" he commanded the waves and the wind.

At once, the wind dropped and the water became calm once more.

Jesus turned to his followers. "Where is your faith?" he asked them. They did not reply. They stared in amazement and awe at this man, who looked just like them, but who gave orders that the wind and waves obeyed. Who could he be, to have such power?

Only believe

MATTHEW: 9; MARK: 5; LUKE: 8

When Jesus returned to the side of the lake, a large crowd was waiting for him. Among them was Jairus, a leader from the local synagogue. He threw himself down in front of Jesus and begged him to return home with him.

"My only daughter is very ill," he said. "She's only twelve years old and is dying."

Jesus set off with the man at once. The crowd followed, jostling him as he went.

In the crowd was a woman, who had been ill for many years. She knew that Jesus had the power to cure her, so she came up behind him and touched his coat. She was instantly healed.

Even though there were many people, bumping against him, Jesus felt the woman's touch.

"Who touched my coat?" he asked.

"Who can say?" replied Peter. "There are so many people around you."

"Someone wanted to be healed," said Jesus, "and they touched me. Who was it?"

When the woman heard Jesus speak, she knew she had been found out. Nervously, she stepped forward and explained why she had touched his coat and how she had immediately been healed.

"Your faith has made you well again," Jesus said to her. "Go in peace."

As Jesus was speaking to the woman, a messenger arrived from Jairus' house.

"Your daughter has died," he said to Jairus. "Do not bother the Teacher any longer."

Hearing this, Jesus said to Jairus, "Do not be afraid. Only believe and she will live again."

They all hurried to the house, where they found everyone outside, weeping.

"Do not cry," Jesus told them. "The girl is not dead. She is just sleeping." He went into her room, took hold of her hand and said, "Get up, child." The girl sat up at once.

"Give her something to eat," said Jesus. The girl's parents were amazed. They could hardly believe what they had seen.

The Good Shepherd

MATTHEW: 18; LUKE: 15; JOHN: 10

All sorts of people came to Jesus and he never turned anyone away. But some of the teachers of the Law grumbled. Why was he mixing with people like tax collectors and wrong-doers? So, one day, to help to explain to them, Jesus told these teachers a story.

"If a shepherd has a hundred sheep," said Jesus, "and one of them gets lost, what would the shepherd do? He would leave the other ninety-nine sheep, safe in the field, and go off to look for the lost sheep. He would not give up looking until he found it.

"Then, the good shepherd would be happy," continued Jesus. "He would lift the sheep onto his shoulders and carry it home, calling to his friends and neighbours to come and celebrate with him, for he had found his lost sheep.

"It is like that in heaven," said Jesus. "I am the Good Shepherd. I have come to look for people, who have wandered away from God, to bring them home to Him. A good shepherd never leaves his flock, even when wolves attack. The shepherd knows every single one of his sheep. The people who follow me are my sheep. I lead them and I protect them. I am willing to give up my life for them."

The seeds that fall in good soil

MATTHEW: 13; MARK: 4; LUKE: 8

Jesus told many stories, or parables, to explain what God's kingdom was like.

"Once, there was a man," said Jesus, "who went out to sow corn. As he scattered it around, some of it fell onto the path. Birds flew down and ate it.

"Some seed fell onto rocky ground. It soon sprouted, but there was not enough soil for it to take root properly. So, when the hot sun came out, the young plants dried up.

"Some of the seed fell among weeds that choked the plants as they grew. And some of the seed fell onto good soil. The seeds grew into healthy plants and produced lots of corn."

Then Jesus explained what the parable meant.

"People who hear God's message, but do not understand it, are like the seeds on the path. They do not accept it. The seeds that fall on rocky ground are like people who are glad when they hear the message, but, as soon as trouble comes along, they give up. The seeds that fall among weeds are like people who let their love of money and other worries smother the message.

"The seeds that fall in good soil are like people who hear what God is saying. The way they live shows that they understand Him and are putting His message into practice."

“I am the farmer…”

MATTHEW: 13

Jesus told another parable to explain about God’s Kingdom.

“A man sowed good seed in his field,” said Jesus. “But, he had an enemy and, one night, when everyone was asleep, the enemy came and sowed weeds among the newly planted seed.

"When the plants started to grow, the farm workers noticed the weeds and asked the farmer, 'Where have the weeds come from? You sowed good seed. Shall we pull them out?'

"The farmer said, 'No! Leave them. You might pull up some wheat as well. When harvest comes, we will get the harvest workers to pull out the weeds first and burn them. Then, we will easily see where the wheat is and be able to gather it and store it in my barn.'"

Later, when the crowd had gone home and Jesus' friends were alone with him, they asked him what the story of the weeds meant.

"I am the farmer, sowing the good seed, spreading the message of God," said Jesus. "The field is the world. The good seed is the people who believe God's message. The weeds are those who belong to God's enemy, the Evil One. The harvest will come at the end of time. The harvest workers are God's angels and they will sort out God's people from those who have turned away from Him or done evil things!"

Five thousand people

MATTHEW: 14; MARK: 6; LUKE: 9; JOHN: 6

As time passed, the crowds, who came to listen to Jesus, grew larger and larger. Jesus spoke for long hours, but time passed quickly, without people realising it. On one occasion, Jesus was teaching by Lake Galilee. At sunset, there was still a large crowd gathered round him. It had been a long day and they were all hungry.

"Send the people away, so that they can go to the farms and villages to find food," said the disciples.

"You, yourselves, should give them something to eat," replied Jesus.

"Where can we go and buy enough food to feed all of these people?" asked the disciples.

Then, the disciple, Andrew, spoke, “Here is a small boy, with five barley loaves and two small fish. But it certainly isn’t enough to feed all these people.”

“Tell the crowd to sit down on the grass,” Jesus told his disciples. He took the bread and fish and thanked God for them.

Then, Jesus gave the food to the disciples, who kept breaking it and giving it to the people. Everyone ate as much as they wanted to. And, when the leftovers were collected, they filled twelve whole baskets.

Five thousand people were fed that day.

Moses and the prophet Elijah

MATTHEW: 17; MARK: 9; LUKE: 9

Jesus knew that word of his teachings was spreading fast. One day, he asked his disciples, "Who do people say that I am?"

"It is said that you are John the Baptist or one of the prophets come back to life," they told him.

"And you?" Jesus asked them. "Who do you think I am?"

"You are the King that God promised," answered Peter. His reply pleased Jesus and he knew that it was time to prepare his disciples for what lay ahead.

"I must travel soon to Jerusalem," said Jesus. "The priests and the teachers of the law do not believe that I am God's Son. They will put me to death, but, after three days, I shall rise and live again."

"If you want to follow me, you must expect hardships," Jesus told his friends. "You must expect to suffer, too."

About a week later, Jesus went up onto a hill with Peter, James and John. As he knelt praying, Jesus' face and clothes changed and became dazzling white.

Suddenly, two other shining white figures appeared – Moses and the prophet Elijah. They spoke to Jesus about God's plans for him and about Jesus' own death.

Peter, James and John had fallen fast asleep. When they awoke and saw the figures, they were very frightened. Then, a cloud passed across the sky and from it, a voice spoke:

"This is my Son. Listen to what he has to say." Then, the vision vanished and Jesus and his friends were alone.

My son was lost

LUKE: 15

Every day, more and more people came to hear Jesus speak, including many outcasts and wrong-doers. The Pharisees, the Jewish teachers of the Laws, were always complaining to one another, “Jesus is not a good teacher. See the bad company he keeps.” So, Jesus told them this story to explain why.

There was once a man with two sons. One day, the younger son said, “Father, I’d like my share of our property.” So the father divided up his wealth and gave one half to each son.

It was not long before the younger son left home and went abroad. He had a wonderful time and, soon, all his money was gone.

Then, famine swept the country and the younger son could only get a job looking after pigs. He was so hungry that he could have eaten the bean pods that he fed to them.

"What am I doing?" he thought to himself. "Back home, even my father's servants have food to spare. Here I am, with nothing to eat. I will go home and admit to my father that I wronged him and God. I will tell him that I am sorry. I do not deserve to be his son, but he might hire me to work for him."

So, he packed up the few belongings that he had and went back home.

The son was still a long way from home when his father saw him. The father was overcome with happiness and rushed out to meet his son. He threw his arms around him and hugged him. The son said sorry, just as he had planned, but his father just called for his servants.

"Bring new clothes," he ordered. "Kill the best calf and prepare a celebration meal. I thought my son was lost, or even dead. But he's alive and he's home again! Let the feasting begin!"

Meanwhile, the elder son had been working away in the fields. As he neared home, he heard the sounds of music and laughter coming from the house.

"What's happening?" the son asked a servant.

"Your brother has come home to us and your father is celebrating," replied the servant. The elder brother was so angry, that he refused to go into the house.

His father came out to see what was wrong.

"All these years, I have worked for you like a slave," he told his father. "And I have never disobeyed you. You have never had a celebration for me, but you do it for that useless brother of mine!"

"My son, you know everything I own is yours," his father said, "but we must celebrate. Your brother was lost and now he's found again."

The good Samaritan

LUKE: 10

Jesus was so popular with the people that the religious leaders became jealous of him. They wanted to get rid of him and some even wished for his death. Others tried to catch him out with difficult questions, such as, “What do I need to do to have eternal life?”

"What does God's Law say you should do?" Jesus asked the leader in return.

"I must love God with all my heart and strength and mind," answered the man. "And I must love my neighbour as much as myself. But what does that mean? Who is my neighbour?"

To answer the question, Jesus did what he often did. He told a story.

"There was once a man, who was on a journey from Jerusalem to Jericho. On the way, he was attacked by robbers. They beat him and left him for dead. Soon after, a priest passed along the road. When he saw the man, he walked by on the other side.

"Then, a teacher of the Law came along," said Jesus. "He did nothing to help the man, either. He, too, crossed over and continued his journey.

"Later, a Samaritan came along. He saw the man and immediately felt sorry for him. He gently cleaned up the man's wounds.

"And with great care, he placed the man on his own donkey and took him to a nearby inn.

"Next day," continued Jesus, "when the Samaritan had to leave, he gave the innkeeper some money and said, 'Take care of this man. When I come this way again, I will pay you any extra that you have to spend.'

"The Samaritan did all this, even though the man was a Jew and the Jews did not like the Samaritans."

Jesus looked at the leader who had asked him the question and said, "Who would you say behaved like a real neighbour?"

"The good Samaritan," replied the man.

"Then go," said Jesus, "and try to be more like him."

The raising of Lazarus

LUKE: 10; JOHN: 11

Jesus liked to visit some friends, who lived in a place named Bethany, near Jerusalem. There were two sisters called Mary and Martha and their brother, Lazarus.

Once, Martha was bustling around, preparing food, while Mary simply sat at Jesus' feet, listening to what he had to say.

"Why don't you tell Mary to come and help me?" Martha said to Jesus, crossly.

"Mary is quite right to listen to me," replied Jesus. "You should not worry so much about worldly things and come and listen to what I have to say, while you can."

One day, Jesus received a message from the two sisters.

"Lazarus is very ill," it said. "Please come to us soon."

Jesus loved Lazarus and his sisters very much, so, naturally, the disciples expected that he would hurry to Bethany. But Jesus stayed where he was for two days, before setting out. He knew that Lazarus, by then, would be dead.

Jesus' friends did not want him to go anywhere near Jerusalem. They knew that his enemies were there, plotting against him. But when they realised that he was determined to go, Thomas said, "Let us all go. We will die together."

As they arrived in Bethany, Martha rushed out to meet them, but Mary stayed in the house.

Martha spoke to Jesus, "If only you had been here, my brother would not have died." By then, Lazarus had been in his grave for four days.

"Your brother will live again," Jesus told her.

"I know that he will live again on the last day," said Martha.

"I am the Resurrection and the Life," replied Jesus. "Whoever believes in me will never really die. Do you believe this?"

"I do, Lord," said Martha. "I finally understand. I believe you are the Christ, God's Son.

"I believe that you have come to give new and eternal life to all who believe in you."

Mary and Martha were so upset that they wept bitterly.

Friends, who had come to comfort the two sisters, were crying too. When Jesus saw this, he was moved and also wept. He had loved Lazarus very much. Seeing Jesus so upset, some people wondered why he had not come sooner and stopped Lazarus from dying.

Then, Jesus made his way to the grave, which was a cave, with a stone covering the entrance.

"Take the stone away," ordered Jesus.

"But, Lord, he has been dead for four days now," said Martha. "There will be a bad smell."

Jesus began to pray. "Dear God. I know that you are my father. But for the sake of the people here, show them a sign that you have sent me."

Then, he commanded, "Lazarus! Come out!"

Immediately, Lazarus walked from the tomb. He was still covered in the cloth that had been wrapped around his dead body.

"Unwind those grave clothes and set him free," said Jesus.

Many people, who were present at this scene, now truly believed that Jesus had been sent by God. But some people did not. They went to the chief priests and told them about the raising of Lazarus. The priests held a meeting.

"Before long," they said, "everyone will believe in this man and follow him. Then, the Romans will think we have started a rebellion."

So, from then on, the priests began to plot Jesus' death.

Have mercy on us

LUKE: 17

On his way to Jerusalem one day, Jesus came across ten men, who had a terrible skin disease called leprosy.

"Have mercy on us, Jesus," the men cried.

"Go and let the priests look at your bodies," Jesus told them. Only the priests could certify that they were truly healed.

As the men hurried to the priests, their skins were healed. One man, a Samaritan, came back to thank Jesus.

"Why has only one man come to thank God, when ten men were healed?" commented Jesus to his disciples. Turning to the man, he said, "Go, your faith has cured you."

Zacchaeus, the chief tax collector

LUKE: 19

Soon, Jesus passed through Jericho. Zacchaeus, the chief tax collector, lived there and he was among the crowd that was trying to catch a glimpse of Jesus. Zacchaeus was quite short and couldn't see over the heads of the crowd. So, he decided to run ahead and climb a tree to get a better view.

When Jesus passed by, he said, “Come down, Zacchaeus. I wish to stay at your house today.”

People were shocked! How could Jesus mix with people like that?

But meeting Jesus changed Zacchaeus.

He offered to give half of his money to the poor and to repay four times as much to those from whom he had taken wrongly.

Jesus turned to the crowd and said, “The Son of Man seeks and saves that which is lost.”

Entering Jerusalem

MATTHEW: 21; MARK: 11; LUKE: 19; JOHN: 12

On the outskirts of Jerusalem, Jesus spoke to two of his disciples.

"Go on ahead of us," he said. "At the edge of the next village, you will find a donkey. Bring it to me and, if anyone asks you why you are taking it, tell them that I sent you and that I will return it to them."

The men found the donkey, threw their cloaks over its back and helped Jesus to climb on.

When the people realised that Jesus had arrived in Jerusalem, they came out to greet him. Some threw their cloaks down in front of him, as he rode along. Others laid down palm branches. "Praise God," they shouted. "God's King is coming!"

On entering Jerusalem, Jesus went straight to the temple. He found it full of men buying and selling doves. Others were exchanging money for special temple coins.

Jesus was furious and began to drive them out. “This is a place of prayer,” he cried, “and you have made it into a den of thieves!”

After this, Jesus healed people who were ill.

When the chief priests heard what he had done, they were really angry. With so many people following Jesus, the priests saw him as a real threat to their power. They were now even more determined to kill him than before.

Thirty pieces of silver

MATTHEW: 26; MARK: 14; LUKE: 22

It was nearly time for the Feast of the Passover. As the disciples bought food at the market, Judas Iscariot crept quietly away to see the chief priests. Evil had entered his heart and he no longer believed that Jesus was from God.

When Judas told the priests why he had come to see them, they were very happy.

"How much would you pay me to give Jesus over to you quietly?" Judas asked the priests.

The priests counted out thirty pieces of silver and gave them to Judas.

"I'll take you to him when he is alone, so that there is little trouble," Judas promised. And from then on, he started to look for the right moment to betray Jesus.

The last meal

MATTHEW: 26; MARK: 14; LUKE: 22; JOHN: 13

On the day before the Passover, Jesus told Peter and John to prepare for the meal.

"But where shall we eat?" they asked him.

"As you enter Jerusalem," replied Jesus, "you will meet a man carrying a water-jar. He will take you to a house with an upstairs room. Prepare everything there for us."

That evening, before the meal, Jesus knew that the disciples had been quarrelling about which of them was the best. So, Jesus calmly took a basin of water and began to wash their feet. Peter was shocked.

"I can't let *you* wash my feet," he said.

"I want you to follow my example," said Jesus. "Whoever wants to be great in the Kingdom of God must learn how to serve others, as I am serving you."

Then, they sat down to eat.

During the meal, Jesus said, "One of you is going to betray me, one who is eating with me now."

Peter whispered to John, "Ask him who it is." And John did.

Jesus replied, "The one who I give this bread to," and he gave each of them a piece of bread dipped in herbs.

So, still they did not know, but later, John remembered that Jesus gave the first piece to Judas and had said, "Go and do what you have to do."

None of the others realised at the time what this had meant. The disciples thought that Jesus was telling Judas, who looked after their money, to go and buy more food. They saw Judas leave the room and knew it was night.

Then, Jesus promised the disciples that God's spirit would always be with them and not to be afraid. He knew that this would be the last meal he shared with them. He took a piece of bread, thanked God for it and broke it into pieces.

"This is my body," he said. "Like this bread, I will be broken. I will die for you. Do this in remembrance of me."

Then, he lifted a cup of wine, thanked God again and passed it round.

"This is my blood," he said. "It will be spilled for many people. Drink it in remembrance of me. We shall not drink together again until we are in God's Kingdom."

A garden called Gethsemane

MATTHEW: 26; MARK: 14; LUKE: 22

After the meal, Jesus climbed up the Mount of Olives with his friends, until they came to a garden called Gethsemane.

As they walked, Jesus spoke to them, "This very night, you will all run away and leave me."

"I would never do that!" protested Peter.

"Before the cock crows," said Jesus, "you will say three times that you do not know me."

"Even if I have to die, I will never say that!" cried Peter. The other disciples agreed.

At Gethsemane, Jesus took Peter, James and John with him, leaving the rest to wait outside.

"My heart is full of sadness," said Jesus. "I must go and pray. Stay here and keep watch." He went a little further and knelt to pray.

"Father," Jesus prayed, "if it is possible, save me from this death, but only if it is your will."

Then, he went back to Peter, James and John and found them fast asleep. He woke them up and asked them again to keep watch. This time, Jesus went deeper into the orchard to pray. Twice more he came back to the three disciples, only to find them asleep again. As he woke them for the third time, Jesus heard the sound of voices and saw the light of torches coming nearer. The temple guards and the chief priests were heading towards Jesus. They had come to arrest him – Judas was leading them.

"The man you want is the man I kiss," said Judas to the guards. He walked over to Jesus and kissed him on the cheek. The guards quickly closed round Jesus, but he did not resist. Peter drew his sword and cut off the ear of the chief priest's servant.

"That's enough!" said Jesus and he reached out and healed the man's ear. Then, he turned to the priests and guards.

“Why have you come armed with swords, as if I were a criminal?” he asked. But the priests and guards marched him off into the night, without a word. Then, all of Jesus’ friends ran away, just as Jesus had said they would.

I do not know him

MATTHEW: 26; MARK: 14; LUKE: 22-23; JOHN: 18

The guards took Jesus to the High Priest's house. Peter followed and slipped into the courtyard. He joined a group of people around the fire. Suddenly, a servant girl noticed him and began to stare.

“Weren’t you with Jesus?” she asked.

“No, I do not even know him,” replied Peter.

Then, a short time after, another person asked him, “Weren’t you a follower of Jesus?”

Again, Peter denied it.

An hour later, a third person said, “You come from Galilee. You *must* know Jesus.”

“No, I do not know him!” cried Peter.

At that very moment, the cock crowed and Peter remembered what Jesus had said. He left the courtyard, broke down and wept.

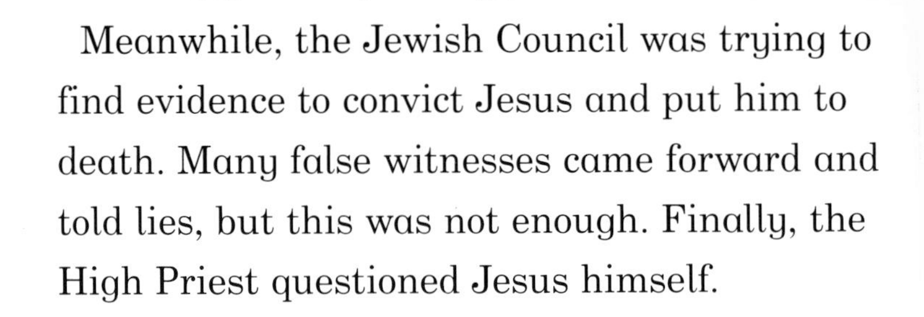

Meanwhile, the Jewish Council was trying to find evidence to convict Jesus and put him to death. Many false witnesses came forward and told lies, but this was not enough. Finally, the High Priest questioned Jesus himself.

"Aren't you going to answer these charges?" he demanded. Jesus did not reply.

"I am putting you under oath," said the High Priest. "Are you the Son of God?"

"You say that I am," said Jesus. "From now on, you will see the Son of Man sitting at God's side."

Furious, the High Priest spoke to the Council. "The prisoner claims to be equal with God," he said. "We do not need any more witnesses after this outburst. What do you think?"

"Guilty!" the Council all shouted. "He must die!"

As soon as Judas heard that Jesus had been sentenced to death, he was overcome with guilt and grief. He went to the priests and threw the thirty pieces of silver onto the floor. "I have sinned!" he cried. "I have betrayed an innocent man." The priests laughed at him. Then, Judas went away and hanged himself.

Meanwhile, Jesus was taken before the Roman governor, Pontius Pilate. The Jews could not execute Jesus without the governor's agreement.

"He claims to be a king," they told Pilate.

"Are you the King of the Jews?" asked Pilate.

"That's what you say," replied Jesus and then he kept silent. He refused to answer any more of Pilate's questions. Pilate could find nothing that Jesus had done wrong and wanted to set him free.

Father, forgive them

MATTHEW: 27; MARK: 15; LUKE: 23; JOHN: 18

It was a Jewish custom to pardon and set free a prisoner at the time of the Passover. Pilate wanted to free Jesus, but the Jewish leaders were determined to get their way.

"Jesus must die," they said. "He claims to be the Son of God, which is against our law."

When he heard this, Pilate was afraid. He ordered that Jesus be whipped. The soldiers made a crown out of thorns for his head and mocked him, saying, "Hail, King of the Jews!" Then, Pilate presented him to the crowd.

"Do you want me to kill your king?" he asked.

"Crucify him!" came the reply. "Crucify him and free Barabbas, instead!"

Then, crying, "Jesus' death is on your hands," Pilate freed the murderer, Barabbas, and the soldiers led Jesus away.

Jesus was forced to carry a huge wooden cross through the streets to Golgotha, the place of execution. As he passed, people mocked him and spat at him. He stumbled and fell and the soldiers ordered one of the crowd, a man called Simon of Cyrene, to carry the cross for him.

A group of weeping women followed Jesus. He turned to them, saying, "Do not weep for me, rather weep for yourselves and your children."

At last, they came to Golgotha. There, guards nailed Jesus' hands and feet to the cross. They nailed a notice above his head, which read, "This is Jesus, the King of the Jews." Jesus was in great pain. The guards offered drugged wine, but he refused. Then, the guards set up the cross, with a thief on either side of him. "Father, forgive them," he prayed. "They know not what they are doing."

The Son of God

MATTHEW: 27; MARK: 15; LUKE: 23; JOHN: 19

People jeered at Jesus, calling out, "If you are the Son of God, come down from the cross and we will believe in you." One of the thieves joined in with the jeers as well.

But the other thief said, "We deserve our punishment. This man has done nothing wrong. Remember me, Jesus, when you come again as King."

"I give you my promise," replied Jesus. "Today, you will be with me in paradise."

Jesus looked down at Mary, his mother, who was leaning on John's arm and said, "Mother, here is your son." Jesus looked at John and said, "Here is your mother." Then, John took Mary away to live in his home.

Beneath the cross, the soldiers were throwing dice to win Jesus' seamless robe.

Suddenly, at twelve o'clock, the sky went dark and a great shadow blotted out the sun. For three hours, there was scarcely any light. Jesus cried aloud, "My God! My God! Why have you left me?" A little later, he called out, "I thirst!" and a soldier soaked a sponge in wine, stuck it on a stick and held it to his lips.

At three o'clock, Jesus gave a terrible cry and said, "It is finished! Father, into your hands, I place my spirit!" Then, he died.

A Roman soldier, who was standing nearby, heard Jesus and said, "This man was truly the Son of God!"

Another soldier pierced Jesus' side with a spear, to make sure that he was dead. Finally, they gently lowered his body down from the cross.

The tomb

MATTHEW: 27-28; MARK: 15-16; LUKE: 23-24; JOHN: 19-20

Later that day, Joseph from Arimathea arrived. He was a follower of Jesus and had permission from Pilate to take Jesus' body away for burial.

Joseph and Nicodemus prepared Jesus' body, according to Jewish custom. They wrapped it in fine linen and special spices and took it to a tomb that had just been dug out of the rock. Mary Magdalene and some other women watched, as a large stone was rolled across the entrance and the tomb was sealed.

The next day was the Jewish Sabbath and the Jews asked Pilate to have the tomb guarded. They remembered only too well what Jesus had said, about rising from the dead!

At sunrise on Sunday, Mary Magdalene and some women returned to the tomb.

When they reached it, they found that the stone covering the entrance had been rolled back and the guards had disappeared.

Inside, the women found an angel.

"Do not be afraid," said the angel. "Jesus is not here. He is risen from the dead. Look, this is where his body was. Go and tell his disciples the good news. You will see him soon in Galilee, just as he promised."

The women, filled with fear and happiness, ran back to tell the disciples.

On hearing the news, John and Peter ran to the tomb and saw the burial clothes lying there. They believed what had been said to them and hurried away, leaving Mary Magdalene weeping by the entrance.

Then a voice asked her, "Why are you crying?"

Mary thought that it must be the gardener.

"Sir, if you've taken my Lord, please tell me where to find him," she said, "and I will go and take him away."

"Mary!" came the reply. It was Jesus! She was overjoyed.

"Go and tell my friends you have seen me," Jesus told her.

Risen from the dead

MATTHEW: 28; MARK: 16; LUKE: 24; JOHN: 20-21

Later that same day, Jesus appeared to two of his followers, as they were walking home from Jerusalem. They did not recognise him and asked him if he would like to eat with them. As Jesus blessed the bread and broke it, the two men realised who he was. Then, Jesus vanished. The two men rushed back to Jerusalem, to tell their friends what had happened.

As the men were telling their story, Jesus suddenly appeared to them all, saying, "Peace be with you." The disciples were really afraid, as they thought they were seeing a ghost.

"See and touch my hands and feet," said Jesus, showing them the nail marks. "Ghosts are not made of flesh and blood."

Then, he sat and ate with them and they knew that this really was Jesus, who was risen from the dead.

Thomas wasn't there that night and when he was told what the disciples had seen, he did not believe it.

"Unless I see and touch the wounds myself," he said, "I will not believe."

A week later, the disciples were gathered together again. Jesus appeared to them and all Thomas' doubts vanished.

The next time Jesus appeared was in Galilee.

The disciples had been fishing on the lake all night, but had caught nothing. In the morning, a man called to them from the shore. It was Jesus.

"Throw out your nets on the right," the man said. "You will make a catch." And he was right!

Then, they ate a breakfast of bread and fish with him on the shore. Three times, Jesus asked Peter, "Do you love me?"

And three times, Peter replied, "You know I do." He knew he was forgiven.

"Then look after my followers," Jesus told him.

The Holy Spirit

ACTS: 1-2

For forty days, Jesus appeared many times to his disciples. They now knew that Jesus had come back to life. But now it was time for him to leave them. So, Jesus led his friends to the Mount of Olives.

"Soon," he said, "God will send you his Holy Spirit. You will be given the power to tell the peoples of the world what I have done and what I will do for them."

As he finished speaking, Jesus was taken up to heaven and a cloud hid him from their view.

Then, two men appeared, all in white. "Jesus has gone to heaven," they said. "He will return one day in the same way you saw him leave."

When the day of Pentecost came, all Jesus' friends met in a house in Jerusalem. Suddenly, the sound of a strong wind came from heaven. It seemed as if flames appeared and touched each of the disciples. They were filled with the Holy Spirit and could speak in languages they had never spoken before. Now they could spread the news about Jesus to everyone.

Jerusalem, then, was full of people from many countries, who had come to celebrate the festival. To their amazement, they heard these men from Galilee, speaking to them in their own languages, about Jesus who had risen from the dead.

Peter stood up and addressed the crowd. He promised that if they were baptised in Jesus' name, God would forgive them their sins. About three thousand people were baptised that day – the Christian Church had begun.

Jesus' friends continued to spread God's word. Their lives were often in danger, but they prayed to God for help and He answered their prayers. Many people came to listen to them and were baptised in Jesus' name.

And today, all across the world, people still gather together to hear God's message.